TESTAMENTS

Miranda Barrett's poems are fierce and penetrating. They cut to the chase, name the unnameable, and wrestle with what matters. And they do so in the name of love. Time and again, she names the pain we bear and still invites us, in her own words, to choose "the creed of kindness." May you steep in the potency of each of these poems.

~ Heidi Rose Robbins, Astrologer, Poet, Author

Poetry invites us to crawl in between the incessant buzzing of our lives to find the quiet spaces, to discover the magic and the meaning. In *The Return Home*, Miranda Barrett gives us the gift of an immense and immediate collection of writing which takes on our collective journeys through the pandemic—and the grief, the love, and the reckoning we all have had to face—and bathes us in a well of compassion and healing. We cannot help but emerge from the reading with perspective and renewed fortitude.

~ Ondi Timoner, Award-winning Non-Fiction Film Director, Producer, Writer

Miranda has ministered to my heart and soul. She is indeed a vessel of truth. She writes from her heart, not her head. Her intention meets that of Spirit and will be delivered to receptive hearts and lives emboldened and empowered to simply live fully and honestly.

The Return Home is not for the faint of heart. Not rated PG. The words cut deeply. I am forever grateful for Miranda being used to deliver this message. Her own life lived that others might thrive.

Reading and ingesting every bit of each poem pulled the mirror closer to the closets closed but not empty, still cluttered and much in need of attention.

The Return Home serves as an intimate excursion through a set of surgery suites. Beginning with Miranda's transparent rendering of a life beset with obstacles into a transformative vessel of light, truth, healing, and spiritual wholeness.

You will experience the surgeon, without scalpel or blade, yet with a ginger unveiling of truth to refine you. Likened to a roller coaster ride of emotions, but a guaranteed sure landing of authentic accuracy. Truly a miraculous delivery, Miranda.

> ~ Marva A. Brannum, Pharm. D. AAHIVP
> Clinical Pharmacist, HIV Specialist

If your Soul is hungry, then prepare to feast on a tasty, fulfilling meal. *The Return Home* speaks specifically to those with the courage to listen, hear, and engage life—reservations and all.

The mystical meditation of words contained within is a healing manual. This healing may not always be apparent because it resides cloaked in the grace of the compassion with which Miranda writes.

There is a silence within her book that courage is born of. These are stories of the freedoms born of fear, growth, and the human struggle for Realization and Enlightenment. Stories that reflect the ancient, within the landscape of the modern, the foretelling and the foretold.

Miranda is what the new Light Warrior Woman Mother looks like: beautiful, strong, soft-spoken, disarming, preparing us with her wisdom-words for the barbarous times at our gates.

Through this poetic journey we can find keys to the Divine parts of ourselves. She writes of love, of self, of woman, of children, mother, father, earth, loss, redemption, the mundane paths to enlightenment, the magical and the mysterious keys to our lofty selves.

Putting her vulnerabilities on the page, you will see Miranda baring herself and challenging us to be more, to be our better selves. Dare to go within!

~ Valdez Flagg, Peabody Award–winning Producer,
DGA Stage Manager

THE RETURN HOME

A heartfelt journey into who you truly are

Offerings by
Miranda J Barrett

Photos by
Megan Barrett

Printed and bound in the United States of America
ISBN paperback: 978-0-9885722-9-4
ISBN hardback: 978-0-9885722-8-7

Dedicated to the truth
that resides within us all
and to my beloveds.

You know who you are…

This magnificent refuge is inside you.

Enter.

Shatter the darkness that shrouds the doorway.

Be bold.

Be humble.

Put away the incense
and forget the incantations they taught you.

Ask no permission from the authorities.

Close your eyes and follow your breath
to the still place that leads
to the invisible path
that leads you home.

~ Teresa of Avila

PLACED INTO THE HANDS OF GOD

FOREWORD BY ED BACON

The stakes are high—life-and-death high—along the all-important journey of discerning what to do in life. Spiritual directors teach what Miranda Barrett, the poet of these pages, expresses. That is, avoiding "desolation" and embracing "consolation" can be very good guides—with a huge caveat. There is such a thing as false consolation if it means that you're feeling good while you are unaware of your complicity in the rape of Mother Earth, a life of self-delusion, and the neglect of children. The latter, Miranda Barrett lyrically and arrestingly calls "the cold ice of emotional disconnect."

In this tour de force of poetry, the reader is treated to both raw trauma as well as potent healing. Barrett is an intrepid Sherpa of sanity who has experienced a way through darkness and disease. Her poems now shine a light on that path. There is indeed such a genuine thing as desolation that wounds us and others and should always be avoided in the journey to maturity that entails fearlessly taking stock and contemplatively undergoing character flaw-ectomy. Miranda also intrepidly describes a desolation that is fueled by love, that refines and distills as it removes all that is not wholeness and grace.

No one rosily "bounces back" to life and health from the valley of trauma Miranda and many of us know. The journey to the Holy Grail she calls her "brand," "Know Who You Truly Are," is labor-intensive. "Labor," rather than "work," is the right word here because Something Sacred, our True Self, our Inner Divine Genius is always being born. Consistently, these poems reveal the requirement of both brave exertion as well as the stillness-induced receptivity of what she calls "the nectar of grace."

This poet has no patience with disembodied truths. Nice and normal make her squirm, as she says. She requires inconvenient, often somatically painful awareness about how we were complicit in distracting and deluding ourselves and thus harming others, the planet, and ourselves. We played a role in the toxification of our own physical, relational, and planetary systems.

Prepare to be arrested by this poetry. This poet's language stops you in your tracks. Speed-reading and transformational poetry do not coexist.

Like all poetry worthy of the name, the poems here invite us to have a personal relationship with them. In order to have a living relationship with a poem, one must slow down to "soul speed." Speed-reading is "ego speed." Putting yourself at the disposal of genuine poetry is "soul speed." Ego speed is also fear speed, while soul speed is love speed. Reading poetry is like life: the speed of breathing, working, thinking, and planning driven by the ego and fear will guarantee that we will exist at the level of the false and superficial self. That superficial level is often as turbulent as the ocean's surface can become. The true self, the authentic self, is the self where the holy makes itself known (who you truly are) and takes place when we slow down to soul speed. Then we visit ocean's depths of centeredness.

A rabbinic friend of mine made it his practice to memorize poems that resonated with him. As a result, his sermons were the most lyrical (as well as courageous) of all the sermons I have ever heard or read. And a fellow listener commented to me after one such sermon, "Leonard just thinks and lives at a level deeper than the rest of us."

The poems in this volume comprise a delivery system for living, thinking, and feeling more deeply than the rest of the world. That is because, as this poet Miranda Barrett makes clear in the book's title, the journey of accessing the energetic whole-making powers of Soul is always a "return home." Soul was our starting place from which we frequently depart—sometimes many times daily. And yet, Soul always stands ready with open arms to welcome us back millions of times over the course of our life. And the welcome is always spread with Soul's banquet. And that banquet is spread in the delicious depths where we touch and are touched by Wholeness.

I call Miranda a personal friend and teacher. I can thereby bear witness that Miranda now dwells in these depths of Soul's banquet of Wholeness. That is not to claim that she is immune to experiences of fear and ego, as well as trauma and brokenness. However, in the midst of these events of real life, her authentic calling is energy healing.

I have personally received her Reiki ministrations with great benefit. My journal entries afterward have a lyricism influenced by the fact that Miranda's parlance and presence are intrinsically poetic. She speaks from Wholeness, invoking wholeness in her clients and friends. The whole thing is poetic, for poetry indeed comes *through* the poet from the center of her (and our) true self which I refer to as Soul, which is Wholeness, which is the Holy in each of us, which is Home.

This book contains great poetry. That is to say that while it delivers on the promise of its title, to return us to the home of our true selves (the God within) both personally and collectively, it also is both timeless and timely. Yeats's "The Second Coming" comes to mind with its description of his time: "the center cannot hold." And yet we use his poem today to language our current appetite for anarchy and democracy on life support. Yeats penned that warning more than one hundred years ago, and we still use it. Miranda Barrett opens this volume with how we have chosen distraction over awareness and how stillness still saves. We will use her words one hundred years from now.

Ed Bacon
October 18, 2021

Priest, Speaker, Author of *8 Habits of Love,* a guest on Oprah Winfrey's Soul Series and one of the most well-known faith leaders in support of the LGBTQ community.

COLLECTIONS

A SPILLING OF VULNERABILITY

Poetry is not for everyone, it seems. My family have been a gorgeous litmus test of this, walking out of the room or refusing to listen to my poems over the years. After deciding not to take this personally, I realized for some people poetry can actually be painful, boring, makes no fucking sense whatsoever, and pierces places they do not want pierced.

I relish this authenticity, and if you're someone who loves poetry, I am thrilled you are diving into this collection. If you are someone who is on the fringes, I welcome your courage and curiosity. My prayer is that I do not disappoint; but hey, if I do, I have to be authentic. I write what flows out of me, not what people like. When I turned forty, I said aloud that I no longer cared what people thought of me. My mother chimed in pretty quickly that I never cared what people thought of me. Spoken by one who knows.

If you are one of those rare creatures who actually hates poetry and yet you are still reading, I salute you with the utmost respect. I will not be offended if, after a few poems, you close the book or take a moment to enjoy the gorgeous photographs taken by my gifted and amazing daughter instead.

These poems spill out of me. Sometimes in very inconvenient moments. Often while sleeping I am awoken by a stirring. I have learned not to ignore putting pen to paper or speaking into my phone. If I do ignore the impulse, sleep eludes me until the deed is done. Once, I was woken from my bed in Vietnam at two in the morning with the inspiration to go find a temple in the village and sit and write in the temple. That poem is in this collection.

These writings are also provoked when I am in nature, often up a mountain, by the ocean, or in communion with other extraordinary beings. A single line in a film may cause a pouring forth. Yet over the years, silence has been my widest, most vast muse.

I have honored this voice of spirit as a representation of my passion for us all to reveal and honor our authentic nature. As a tonic to cure the trauma and the wounds we carry in our bodies from the past.

Sometimes I write a word which I do not know the meaning of and have to look it up later. For me, this is a living testimony that these poems flow through me, leaving me with a curiosity of where they came from. This is an act of service, a seeming gift from the divine.

I would say I am close to being a virgin in this world of creative writing, even though I wrote my first poem at the age of twelve. I am in awe of the poets through the ages and their extraordinary gifts of being such instruments of words. I have never paid much attention to grammar, sentence structure, or punctuation. Still don't ... apologies to my editors. So it is with some reticence that these ducklings are being birthed into the world. Yet, here we are.

I am continually surprised by these poems which fall out of me. Also forever grateful and humbled, if not slightly confused. The capacity for my own transformation in their healing presence and as footsteps on my own journey.

There seems to be a potency in this form of metaphor which touches deep below the surface.

This collection is an unfurling of my internal world which I hope resonates with yours. As we know, when one person dies, we all die a little. We are all tethered. We are all connected.

I am not a religious person, yet am deeply devotional. These poems are my prayers. I hope they become yours. I hope they bring solace to your heart. I hope they quiet the insanity of your mind and thoughts. I hope they bring you back to love and compassion for yourself and thus others. I pray this can be a tiny drop of healing in this wounded world of ours.

Now a word or two about vulnerability. I am English. I was brought up in a boarding school. Being rendered vulnerable, exposed, talking about feelings is everything I was trained not to do. So, when I say this is a calling, it is! It is my higher nature overriding all the parts of me screaming, "No! Do not publish this book. Do not expose your underbelly. Do not give people ammunition." It goes against the grain of my privacy, my wounds, all that wants to protect the truth and not reveal it. Yet here we are. I am launching this precious inner world of my own story. But more importantly, revealing a pathway of restoration I have been honored to witness in service to others.

While I do recognize that our individual journeys are unique in mysterious and harrowing ways, over time I have noticed a universality in the healing of the human psyche, the human body, and the human spirit. This gathering of poems

3

speaks to this. With a beckoning door opened to touch a part of us which has remained hidden, compartmentalized, and a stranger all these years.

My prayer is that this sea of words can be received as a healing manual to provoke our own capacity to love more. To love ourselves, to love others, to love this precious earth. In so doing, to reveal our own unique way of loving and in turn recognize the merciful and redemptive love in others.

This gift of vulnerability, this gift of thousands of swirling words is offered as a pilgrimage of remembering for you. As the title echoes, if you soften and listen deeply, you can receive these poems as a way forward.

For you to return home to the nature of your being. To the authentic, most beautiful, radiant, glorious self who is already within you and is waiting patiently at the door to greet you.

"When you were born you were crying
and everyone else was smiling.
Live your life so at the end,
you are the one smiling
and everyone else is crying."

~ Ralph Waldo Emerson

LOVE AWAITS

Pick a poem, any poem, and let it walk you home.

Open the book at any page and see what Spirit is telling you.

Read a poem to your loved one, your clients, at a retreat, in circles, to your children. (Just don't pick from deep, dark waters and scare your children. My prayer is that they are having a wonderful childhood.)

Explore the book cover to cover. While birthing this creation into form, I was guided to deliver the collection as a pathway for healing. Hence, if that calls to you, I would offer that you read from the beginning over a spaciousness of time. Pause on the one poem which rattles you to the bone or allows a ray of hope. Read it a second time. These writings are a journey. An opportunity to begin again, be birthed anew, and heal the wounds carried from the past.

HOLY WORDS

Sit a while, dear one, to become your own compass

Breathe this moment in to gather yourself home

Begin this quest, a ritual walking with Spirit

Let Divine Mother embrace you

Let all Saints behold you

The Sages lead you

The Yogis bless you

The Prophets adorn you

Let the treasure house of light befriend you

Let Buddha nature awaken you

Christ consciousness stir within you

Mysticism anoint you

The ancestors protect you

The universe respond to the heart of you

Let an army of consciousness guide you

Pray the confines of spirit be unleashed in service to you

Grace bestow you

Dearest beloved one, this is my prayer for you

MOMENTS OF REFLECTION

The racing mind
spun
out of control
Desperate to keep up with the fears
The narrative of internal horror stories

Spinning to quell the terror
The demands
The endless list

A whirling life
A wooden top
Round and round
inhaled by a frantic need

to not land in the present moment
to not feel
the still quiet motionless hum of now

More to do
Spin faster
Bypass what is

Prophesying the future
Dissecting the past
Spinning on its own axis
A frenzied hunger to devour itself

The root touching the earth
Yet the motion

out of control
out of our senses
The dread of the shattered pain
rises up
from below the surface of the path
paved with reticence

Keep thinking
Keep spinning
Scheming
Thickening the plot

Aligning with the madness
Fighting reality

What is this heart
Disappointed
Let alone to feel deeply

To allow every and each tendril of loss to wither on the vine
Destroying the precisely placed tiles on the roof of protection

Thy will be done
This surrender
a distant memory
of sanity

What we ask might appear
if the loving finger of the universe
with devotion
lightly touched
the tip of the wooden top

Calming the child
Pausing the momentum
Crashing the façade
The scaffolding of delusion

In that moment
A break would appear
A wrinkle in time
A pause to wonder

A life in motion
Halted
Returning to truth
To stillness
To quiet
To reflection

What then
What now
What fun!

Relinquish the old currencies

Undeclare yourself
into all that you have believed to have known

Swim in the darkening waters of vulnerability
The disappearance into intimacy's enfolding arms

Into what is becoming
To stand still in this moment now

Nothing hauling you from your center
No story to tell
No ego to build
No reality to shatter

Nothing pulling you apart
No more swirl
to lose yourself in

Let your own hand of God
Lovingly place
with a touch of devotion
the crown of the head

Bring your own self to stillness
Stop your own pivot
Ground your feet
Calm the exhausted mind

Be come still
Be come quiet
Do nothing
Be nothing

Breathe into the pause
of all momentum

Let simple awareness be the orchestra
The music to still your soul

and in this pause of frenzy
be curious

Who is home
without the twist

Who are you
without the churning of the mind

What is it you are needing

Choose this very moment

Now

As a chance to turn your life around

To face the stranger within

Turn back into stillness
Return to silence
Remember who you truly are

"As I begged the wise one
to tell me the secret of the world
Gently
she whispered
'Be quiet
The secret cannot be spoken
It is wrapped in silence'"

Last paragraph by Rumi (adapted)

"The Kingdom of Heaven
is spread upon the earth,
but humans do not see it."

~ Jesus

THE HEART OF THE MATTER

Sacred encounters
while walking this blessed earth

A TIMEOUT

If it feels like we have been given a timeout
well we have

We have been sent to our corners
Driven back to our internal world
Returned to stillness if we choose

The still point
where we can no longer cause havoc
damage or destruction.

We are refugees returning home to our own internal worlds

To see what we are made of
To exceed our capacity
To embody our resilience

In a time
where we can no longer use our drugs of choice
as distraction

The plea bargain is over
The river has dammed
The currents of
stress
achieving
production

The overuse of our world
our nervous systems
Now we get to sit in the waters of our own making
Motionless in the reality
as brutal truths are revealed

A stark reckoning
of having skin in the game

Without discernment
this has become an island of fear
Hatred and division the religion

These are pregnant times
To know who we are

Spiritual warriors in times of crisis
When all else comes to a grinding halt

Yes a timeout
Yet also a time to choose
Awareness or distraction
Surrender or control
Faith or fear
Discipline or apathy

Neither can hold the same breath

What does it mean when guns
cannabis
toilet paper
are where we turn

Gather what you value
Your truth
Your solace

Dive deep
Look hard
Become still

To reveal what lies beneath the surface
that has drowned our world

THE BELL TOLLED

A startling
awakening
of truth

A distillation
etched
in choices made

Conscious or unconscious
The decisions from yesterday
The actions of years gone by
born of familiarity
result directly
in where I stand today

Each option chosen
builds a trajectory
a path trodden
a way forward

These choices
now give isolation
quarantine
a flavor
a taste
of their very own making

Where I am
in life
in relationship

with others
with myself

These actions of the past
land squarely
imprinted
branded on this present time

Nowhere to run
tethered in footprints
caught in this web

Concrete slabs of
comfort
fear
habit

Always summoning
Always becoming

The same old tracks run their course

But what if a different future is beckoning
A return to a virgin state
where the path to such unfolding
is in making different decisions in the now

What if
authenticity
courage
surrender
became the superpowers

What if
the decisions made in this moment
crystallized in awareness
set the future free

What if the shackles that imprint
the limitations
the ruins
heartache
dragged with disdain from the past into the present
were laid to rest
burned to the ground
cindered to ashes

The past liberated
forgive
forgiven
and forgiven
some more

Until nothing is left
A void
penniless
unable to drag the past into the future

Then choices in the present
become the true temple of authority

A steward of volition
A governor of actions
become sovereign to the moment now

Whatever is given
time
investment
attention
is the direction becoming

Preferences made
without the haunting stories of the past

This will foretell the future

This will make a different future

This will let the future free

MY CREED IS KINDNESS

In a world turned to hate
Where division bleeds from the tit
Where ignorance feeds prejudice
Where fear feeds isms out of control

A country built on rivers of blood
stolen lands
genocide
slavery

Religion force fed
down the throats
of those
who understood
nature is the religion

Lives taken
Tribes destroyed
Ways of life vanished

Hungry ghosts haunt this land

The heartbeat slows
The blood
running through the veins
turned cold

Old ways never healed
never acknowledged
never changed

A drumbeat of domination and control

Blood soaks the earth
Staining the streets

Violence steeped in aggression
bloodies the eyes

The poison airborne
The hatred palpable

A virus born
A potent opportunity to care
A revolution to unite

Yet in this reckoning
we the people
divide more

The united states
torn and tattered

Stars and stripes
crippled in shreds

No longer hanging
in the hope
of honor
decency

The legacy is shame
This reality survived by millions
for hundreds of years
yet lived unconscious by the rest

This is not new
Only now the veils have lifted

Technology gives rise
Snuff films to watch
Our own breath taken away
The names not said
The lives already taken
always is
always was
always has been

Appetites
gone wild
out of control

A greed turned rancid
A constitution distorted
A legion of errors
A torrent of domination

Animal nature
exhausted to the bone

This inheritance
left to the children
A wasteland lies ahead

The voice of the grandmother
Honey kills more flies than vinegar

For change
For hope

For transformation

I choose kindness

I choose this as my creed
as a ripple of hope
for this world

EARTH'S MENOPAUSE

Mother Nature
The earth mother from whence we came
The womb of our existence
The haven needed to survive

Yet no longer can she be mother with adults gone wild
No longer can we suck on her tits with abandon
Stomp across her fallow belly
with disrespect
with greedy
torrid
tiny childlike hands
scratching and crawling for more

Never looking her in the eye
Ever noticing the exhaustion wiped across her face
Too many years without appreciation
for the generous bounty of her heart

Defiling extremities
With a heaving sigh she finally lays down the role of sacrifice
Nothing left to bleed

Earth is no longer mother
Earth, she has entered menopause

Gone from maiden
when her innocence was treated with respect
Rhythms held sacred
Rituals honored in her seasons

All who lived within her union
In relationship
In knowing we were one

This virgin earth unfolding
into the pregnancy of humanity
The tenuous role of sacrificing nurturing mother

Teaching discipline through consequences
Yet the lessons remain unlearned
The results dire
The cause and effect on steroids
Too many years in the making
Too many years parenting children refusing to mature

The responsibilities of the mother
never able to graduate into the hands of the grown up

A forced menopause
stimulated by blunt force trauma to her earth

The masculine now rises in tandem
To hold the weight of authority
with domination and control
No more hemorrhaging the bloodline of the universe
The father takes up arms
The one who kicks the baby bird out of the nest

No longer will she hold us to her breast
Feed us
Nurture us
Forgive us our sins
The weaning is complete

Too much taken
Adolescence on fire
Her menopausal heat is rising
Sloughing off the mantle of clothing called humankind
Cracks form in the night sweats of terror
Her body wrinkles
Dry tenuous caverns become the deathly fall
Emotions rise
Waters spill
No more tolerance for childish behavior
Selfishness gone rancid
The crone has risen

Once brimming with fertility hormones
to afford her own slaughter
Earth mother has grieved
Now she fights
She will claim herself back with or without us

Do not mess with a woman in a menopausal body
Never piss off a witch on fire
The banshee unleashed
She is already burning too bright
The body already free
Already transformed
No longer meant for procreation
The disillusionment of needing to please
The instinct to protect or enable the insanity unbearable
The desire to adapt some more lost to the winds of time
Attraction no longer the currency
Authenticity now the creed

She is no longer in service to others
The earth is claiming her own
Claiming her birthright
Returning home to her bounty
Shaking off the minions living on her back

The knife edge to the heart
The threat real
The choice
The action
To honor and respect her evolution
or remain emotionally unintelligent creatures
Whining
spoilt
bleeding her dry
Until the last whisper of breath is our own demise

Her womb is no longer home
The children grown
It is time to respect the parent
To honor the elder
A new age to care for what was so carelessly taken for granted
Sacred earth will no longer tolerate what we have become

Turning her face back to the moon
Her faith back to her gods
planets
galaxies
The cherished fallen from the center of the universe
Reality finally defines what is real
She will not tolerate the rape
or be mistreated in an abusive relationship
The reckoning of a divorce

Now her time to ignore us
To rise up in her glory
In her might as a force of nature
To let us know she will no longer abandon
her body for our selfishness

We took her beauty for granted
Her generosity for granted
Her patience for granted

We took all that has been gifted to us
Exploiting all that we never earned
gravity
sunshine
oxygen
vegetation
the cycles of creation
destruction

All these anointings
discarded by the darkest corners of our hearts

What has become of the traditions
The cultures devoted to her
Who honored the mother
Who gave back more than they took
Who offered ceremony for her gifts

Who were destroyed by greed
Blinded by instant gratification
Delusional in the belief she would always be home

No investment can increase
unless lived with appreciation
This endowment of earth not only ignored
but spent recklessly
Now in the red
This contribution is dying a death for us all

This menopausal earth, she will carry on
Uncaring what others think
Resigned in the survival of her children
Relentless in her own becoming
Liberated in her own undoing

Kiss the hag on the mouth
No longer caring about her beauty
Chasms deep within her potent womb
severing all that is sacred

Mother earth
An ambassador of love
A steward of us all
We have become too many
Too hungry

No longer following nature's laws

As she traverses her eclipse
This stage of life
Nature bound
She is claiming her transition into the crone
Wise woman
The one who silently and fiercely knows

We can no longer ignore this tremendous earth
Her symptoms
Her unfurling
The illness
This shattering death march no more

Earth is in menopause
She no longer prays for us
as we have forgotten to pray for her

She no longer sacrifices for us

Yet to survive

Now we must sacrifice for her

BARE KNUCKLE FIGHTER

Years in the making
Delusion the general at the helm
Baying to the storytellers
The fighting words scribed inside the skull
The vision distorted
upside down in reality
Yet the brain loyal to the lie

Poisoned crow feathers
scarred deep within the lesion
Buried
beyond the reach of sanity

The stench torrid
in the depravity of the wound

as the full moon
falls from the sky

The child soldier
provokes the fight
Drenched in scar tissue
dripped with blooded war paint
Ashes of the ancestors
covet the flesh

The war cry heard
An echo
in the hidden valley of the heart
The fight is on

The arena
hands of trauma
encircle the howling beasts of truth

Bare knuckles
The body exposed
No rules heralded
The gladiators' ring on fire

The body braces
Shoulders hunched
The southpaw breaks its step

Teeth clenched
in a battle against the truth
This enemy creates
a new creed

Truth unhoods its form
The terror
The enemy of shadows
which breaks the spell
of all illusion

The dance begins
The terrified child
throws the first punch

The fist hits the air
Dissolves
as no separation remains
Flailing into nothingness
as the truth has no fight

No real enemy
No defense
Never has
Never will

It just simply is

Reality resting in the truth
of its own sovereignty
The call to arms
stirs silent echoes
which exist no more

The final frontier of authenticity
With nowhere else to turn
Nowhere to hide

The tiny hands thrash into the void
Fighting phantoms of the past
The sincerity stands in stillness
Martial art in the making
Patient in waiting
Loving in stance
An omen
as the clenched fist harbors truth's sentient being

Knowing in time
exhaustion
from this crusade against reality
will lay the child down
Wasted
into the cradled arms of support

Conscious at last
there is no way to win

This tapping out
The first blush of surrender

MERCURIAL FLIGHT

Density weighs down the body
A grounded invasion
embodied in ways of unfamiliar discomfort
A gravity blanket laid heavy across all realms of the body

The brain becomes pudding
Doubt spiraling
Clouded confusion with eyes still open

Sleep eluding
The viral snake moves throughout the body
DNA on fire

Organ to organ
Palpable in touch

The intuitive guidance
Keep the vaccine moving
Reiki the medicine
Visualization the radar
Transmute into an ally
Not to let it stagnate
Take hold
Grow roots

Calling on the alchemists of the ages
Calling on those
who could transmute mercury through the body
and release without harm

These Siddhis available
Intention honed in consciousness
The power of Reiki to do no harm
The alchemical world of healing
Transformation of matter

The toxins collected in tiny mercurial balls
Gathered
Guided
Released
To be neutralized
Transfigured into protection
The dross freed from whence it came
Poured back into the earth
Into existence

With gratitude receiving the antibodies
The rest sloughed off
Just as the bleeding wall
of the uterus releases her charge

THE SILENT WAR

When the enemy behind your back
is unseen
A vaporous hollow
of manipulation
algorithms

When the prey
does not know it is being stalked
There is no defense
The enemy sugarcoated in addictive stickiness

When this becomes the war zone
The battlefield fighting hidden ghosts
Phantom limbs lost to the fight

A sense of dread
Knowing the terrain unsafe
Intuition finally raises her voice
Not knowing which way to run

Ropes become serpents
Feelings gone rogue
Thoughts the monsters of narrative
The brain on fire
The real threat shattered into a fractured mirage
A kaleidoscope colored by fantasy

Numbing with substance
Dissolving into technology
Lost into worlds
where the eyes
hands

breath
forced down tiny electronic tunnels of delusion

The war unfettered
The enemy able to breach every door
Its weapon
technology
Its arsenal
fear
The ammunition
not wanting to feel

Every psyche splayed open
An infiltration of invasion
Bait for the fisherman
Prey for the hunter

The puppet strings controlled by a few
Human intent gone rancid with greed
Perverted with power
Dissolving the middle path
The cascade of the mighty
ripping open the division of the masses

No war cry heard
No sirens sounded
The warning silenced in delusion
The contorted belief
the threat is not real

No bomb shelters built
No rationing upheld
Living as though there is peace on earth
As though earth is not in combat

Yet on the front line of reality
Truth lies fallow
bleeding on the inside
Apocalyptic wounds seep within the fragile psyche

The battle rages on
Do not waste the kill
Laid waste
suicide leaves its mark
War is at every doorstep
Danger in every home
Threatening every age

What general do we turn to when there is no leadership
The alphas gone mad
The authority unstable
The waif in dark waters takes up the reins
Pushes back against the pack
Tries to take the lead

Yet with an invisible gun held to the chest
No separation between you and the enemy
Russian roulette
spins the barrel

Yet the bullet
the bullet is real

while the phantom limbs continue to feel

A FUNERAL PYRE

Although the funeral is over
the world of hurt remains

The cavernous separation
Each one of us colonized
in the deceit of history

The lethal myths of god's work
Masking human greed
Domination
Control

Our humanity torn asunder
The canyon cracks its levee
The divide breaks
fracturing embers of truth
A cascade molten from the fire

Lean into the pain
Surrender into the shock
Soften into the trauma

Become aware of
the capacity of human cruelty
In hope
remember
the capacity of human decency
Know this ragged edge
lives within the heart of us all

No longer avoid facing your own shadow
The hellacious voices in the head
The vitriolic judgments of others
Explore this underworld

There is a war
raging within us all right now

A righteous war
A battle which needs
to be brought up
from the shadows

Choose who you are in this fight
Internal silence your guide
To distill down
into right action

Know who you are
Know your truth
Know what you value
Make an altar of life

No longer lie silent in avoidance

Call forth intuition
Guard her boundaries with your life
Your deepening internal compass of
knowledge
wisdom
This the messenger of salvation

Educate yourself
Notice your complaints
Use this life force for change
Out of respect for what you value

And then stand

Stand up

Take action

Speak up

No more living in denial
Swimming in waters
stained with blood
of our own making

Stand tall in knowing who you are
Stand strong
Committed to what is most important

Reclaim your agency

Start with loving kindness
to understand yourself

Restore faith for your loved ones
The young
The innocent
The stranger

Pour forth into your family
Your beloveds
Your community
Your neighborhood
Your work
Your precious world

Let the embers of this fire fan a new way

The breath
The voice
be the bellows

This phoenix is rising
Her screech fills the air
Her wings fuel the flames
Her devotion
to bring us back to our senses

Feed the right fire
Provoke the activist
Restore the one awake and alive

Nurture consciousness over hatred
Incite love over fear

Commit to what you know to be true
Commit to your deepest heartfelt truth
Let your mind be of service to your heart

Open your eyes and see
Open your ears and listen
Open your mouth and speak
in a stand for justice

In silence we are complicit
In nonaction we are complicit

The time is now
The moment is now
Time the most precious
yet limited commodity we have
Never to be recovered

Stand up
Wake up

Shed the lethargy
The delusion
The avoidance
Shed the lethal injection
The torrid belief this is not your concern

We are all connected
We are all humanity
We are all part of this earth

We are in a great pause
A pandemic to repair the destruction of equality
To burn strong

To shine bright against prejudice gone viral

Turn your head in the direction
you do not want to turn
Take the step you do not want to take
Shackle your complacency

Cross the threshold
shimmering between these veils

We are citizens of two worlds
Walk between what is hidden
Fall deep into your spiritual nature
to show the way as a guide
Take action with your human nature
to restore partnership
Become a ripple of good in these realms
In thought
In word
In deed

Release the illusion this is not your responsibility

We are a tapestry
Every thread vital
Each stitch a part of the weave

Experience the funeral pyre
Yet make it not yours

This is not just a funeral

Where food is brought
Attention given
Hugs administered
Time offered
Kindness in the community lasting but a few weeks
Until the carcass is buried
The ashes scattered
The casserole rots in the fridge

Stay awake
Bring your precious time
Your valuable attention
Your priceless resources

The funeral
only the beginning of grief
for all which is lost
never to be found

Let us not bury our humanity
Let us not destroy our world
Let us not burn to an ash
humankind

Do not go back to sleep

The price is devastation

Stay awake

No longer complicit in silence

"Truly, it is in the darkness
that one finds the light,
so when we are in sorrow,
then this light is nearest of all to us."
~ Meister Eckhart

MERCY

Attend to grace,
brimming in the wisdom of grief

A REQUIEM OF GRIEF

Grief
She will have her way with you
Wrapping you in fiery arms of despair
Destroying the tendrils of your heart
The logic of your mind
The structure of your body

A fist to the soft underbelly

Her fingers will grip your throat
Burn your lungs
Steal the air you breathe
Wailing her unfettered cry

There is no negotiation
She will burn you to the ground
Bring you to your knees

A primal moan will peel itself from your core
Unleashing what was never known before

A banshee keen
Lit from the inside
Writhing
A snake caught on fire
Nowhere to go
Nowhere to run

The bitch is at work
The fire running wild

You are her course
Her fuel
She will not be burned out
until her labor is done

Fire will meet fire in a crescendo of emotion
Beyond mortal in its power

Devastating to the ego's delusion of control

The ultimate fear made manifest
So human in this night terrors of loss
Let the fire of grief course through your veins
Let her ravage every valley
every mountaintop

She will eventually have her way with you
She will not play fair
She will not shoot straight

Her fight is pure and dirty
To burn your attachment back to ashes

Let her hold you in her iron grip
Surrender to the fight
She will always win

She will devour you in her greed for righteous sorrow

It is her creed

Let her burn your whole house down

BLACKENED HEART

Grief simply a portal to love
A declaration of love no longer able to express itself
The object of its affection
lost to death
endings
separation

The love trapped
Snared
Circling the heart
Catching in the throat
Numbing the mind

The arms no longer able to cradle
The words no longer an audience
Hands no longer able to touch
Lips and cheeks no longer there to kiss

Devotion no longer afforded

Grief
blackens the heart

Until
a flicker of light
far in the distance

The light of unconditional love
The truth

Love resides
even in death
even in loss
defying the human terror of annihilation

Even with eyes wide open
grief never seen coming
Impaling the senses

Yet love defies it all
Grief the messenger of love
of how deeply you care
The more you grieve
the richer the torture

Courage comes from the heart
Love comes from the heart
Woven into the tapestry of being

To absorb the bitter taste of grief
To digest her nectar
To drink her blood
To breathe deep
into the death
of sorrow's embrace

The atonement
The blacker the grief
The deeper the love

IF LOVE WAS ENOUGH

If love was enough
I would stay
I would be here now

This bag of bones would have survived
A miracle would return
If love was enough

If love was enough
to stitch the wound
stop the pain
heal the disease
return to health

If death had not come in her dark fury
shrouded in time

If the explosion of love for you in my heart
broken into a thousand pieces
could banish death
in the light of hope

Sending healing to the cells
Sealing the hemorrhage of the blood

This ravaged body would obey my heart
My love
My desire to be well

To be with you
To not die
If only love was enough

Tired to the bone
The silent bleed of life force would stop
Sutured by love
If love could cure the wound
Heal the body

If my love for you was enough
I would be here now
With you
Always

If love was simply enough

"The past and present wilt.
I have fill'd them, emptied them.
And proceed to fill my next fold of the future."
~ Walt Whitman

A MEMOIR

Deepening dark waters

WHO AM I

This question
An old favorite of mine

I am disciplined with my body
yet have taken years to embody her fully
A crest of a heart
was bestowed as a birthmark to my cheek
A constant reminder to return to love
It seems I do not need drugs for altered states
Silence is my muse
Love my creed
Truth my north star
Freedom my devotion
Paradox my undoing

An honor of my work is officiating weddings
yet have never had the desire to marry
unless you count union with the divine
Another paradox indeed

Nice and normal makes me squirm
Eccentric
unorthodox
authentic makes my heart soar

The Joker and the Fool are my favorite cards
Toads and stags my spirit animals

If I love you, I will love you fiercely
Fight for you
Die for you

My heart has loved deeply many times
Also shattered into a thousand pieces
to expand more

My wounds have begged for healing
My actions for forgiveness
My soul for mercy
I lead with silent footsteps
I have been blessed with teachers of distinction
and continue to be so

Feathers and antlers are my friends
as are beauty
spaciousness
devotion

My home a living altar
Prayer my most favorite language
The fire of spirit my love affair
Meditation my return home

I walk between two worlds
with a confused tilt to my head at times
I am loyal to a fault

Prejudice makes me physically sick
I bow deeply to courage
There will be laughter in my presence
sometimes tears

I feel swearing is an art form
I love this earth
Nature is my church
Flatlands disturb me
Mountains give a sense of home
I seem to attract wild animals
in a Snow White kind of way

Truth is my ally
Lies break my heart

I embrace the shadow as an old friend
My commitment is to always dissolve back to love
To surrender to consciousness unfolding

I have deep respect for emotional intelligence
A good hug my idea of heaven
I have a dislike for punctuation
I find it hard to remember names
yet a face is engraved forever
I love psychic intervention
I love original creative rebellion
To lead others into the spirit realms
Into the fury of passions unleashed

I love to dance between the veils
I meet thresholds
simply as a beckoning doorway to walk through

Spiritual bypass makes my lip curl
I have been known to growl
I am devoted to the healing of the ancestors
I am a fierce mother, which has been my greatest joy
I am a daughter
A sister
My beloved friends are my chosen family

I listen deeply to the voice in my head
Some may call this insanity
Yet I am blessed to be touched
by a madness of intuition

My weakness a good whiskey
I roll a mean cigarette
Celibacy often calls my name
until my Scorpio nature is provoked
My journey is to experience it all as sacred

This a smattering of Miranda

Who am I

I am who

All that I do not know

Much of my ego's mantle
Filled with corrosive doubt
In the unleashing of this static
Released back into a gateway of mystery

I am...

What if I just left it there

With the possibility
these poems reveal the truth of my nature
without a label
without conditioning
without having to prove a thing

MOTHER

I bow to the gift of my life
An honoring of the one who carried me in her womb
Birthed my body at the stroke of midnight
In a corridor
of the namesake Battle Hospital

On bended knee
I meet with compassion
the fears and traumas
living wild within your pregnant body

With heart splayed open
I acknowledge the pain within you
The harrowing experience of your own childhood
which never received the nurturing mother
Devoid of safety
Stability extinct

With palms in prayer
I recognize the neglect pouring through the ages
From one generation to the next
Yet a life was always given
An embryonic seed of potential

To be born
To be realized
To continue this offering of life

For a time our connection only lived through sorrow
A torrid remembering

Cradling the pain body in loving arms
The heavy fates and destinies
Returned to the ancestors who bore the trauma

Given back with love
Released through forgiveness
It is all set free

For the future generations to live unshackled
by the haunted ghosts of the past

Rather I take all your love
I receive all your care

I thank you for your blessing
I thank the ancestors for their blessings
as I do life differently

I thank you for your own healing

I thank you
for this precious gift of my life

THE MOTHER OF ALL WOUNDS

Born and bled
with hearts ripped open

The retribution of the matriarchal ancestral line

The wretchedness
Torrid
Pouring forth through the ages

The pain body lies
Unhinged
Unhealed
Raging
Ravaging the tender coils
of innocence born and lost

The heavy fate or destiny
of that not seen
or touched
or ever healed

Secrets
Scarred deep in the folds of the womb's lining

Branded through the psyche
Scorched by pain

Held in rough blistered hands
devoid of love's balm

Nursed with nipples of pain
blood red
dyes the milk
An energy of vampire's delight
A sperm implodes an egg

These children of children
unprepared for the rapture

Hearts steel to love
bleed into the edges of motherhood

Paper cuts
thin slices of love
tear at the heart

Emotions raping the soul
Hormones boiling
Blistering the depths
of the new sleep deprived mother

These children broken from their own mothers
Become the belly of creation and destruction

A responsibility born into the lap
devoid of any manual

The child raises the child

The wound disciplines the innocent
The narcissist captures the mirror

Hungry ghosts haunt
the archetype of Mother

Resentment builds
as the shattered spirit battles the self sacrifice
a good mother would demand

The starving empty void has no desire to give
what she is already lacking

Trapped in the reflection of her own starvation
Bleeding wounds
collide to become a bloody mess

The child also caught
in between the cracks of dementia
Forgotten love
Absence of heart
of tenderness

Hecate born of Mother
Kali devouring the young
A mother rat eats her children to ensure survival

We test the womb for fertility
the hormones
the body

Who tests for the capacity to love
before creation begins

And what of you
who were mothered by a teenage rebellion

What of you
who shape shifted your soul small
to fit into the mold

What of you
who used frogs as protection

What of you
who are never enough
or too much in the same breath

What of you
The one with an inner strength
who can embrace gratitude for this gift of life

What of you
who calls forth
all who suspended this miracle of you

You who lay gratitude at the altar of the ancestors
with eyes wide open
Fists unclenched
for the first time

The newborn turns to the light
Her face towards the smell of mother
Her heart yearns to belong
to be nestled

Yet knowing the wound of mother
has poured through the ages
Each mother broken
battered by the mother before
Each did not receive the devotion needed
The fountain of unconditional love
derailed
distorted

as the pain body
made her new way

Give back this pain
This trail of rejection
neglect
abandonment
manipulation
Implore the mother of all wounds
the ancestors
unapologetically to take back their torment
their heavy fate

Call on
the domain of Mother
the Mother of all mothers

The Divine Mother

Beseech her blessing
For grace to rain down
in storm clouds of purification

Again and again and again

As you live your life as a woman
As you live your life differently
to what was done before

And what of you
If you loved and loved and loved yourself
in the way you have longed for
prayed for
dreamed of

And what of you
If you parented
embodied
nurtured
the infant innocence of you

Let this mantle be the new echo
A ripple of love
like you have never been loved before

MARK OF THE BEAST

Birthed
into a corridor
of light and shadow

With the mark of the beast
A kiss from God
A dent for the ego
in the transcendent shape of love
Lying stretched
for all to see
across the cheek

An infant let alone
The tired
The hungry
Waiting
Writhing into a silenced howl
For touch
For love
For food

A fall into graceless emptiness
Alice took the potion
The looking glass shattered
Energy courses through the veins
A fire spills up the spine
Burning steel horizons
Scorching the psyche

The physical body expands
The energy mountainous
as the room diminishes
Alice caught on fire
Trapped in the bottle

Spirit takes its hold
The hand of the divine
squeezes her magic
to shrink the body immeasurably small

A dissolving of form
Released back into a dot of existence
To implode into the void
Floating
nothingness
yet pregnant with it all
Again and again

The young child awakens
Cheek pressed to cold tile
on a bathroom floor
A collapse back into the body
A crash landing
Seared into the senses
Into the realms of humanity
A fever pitch of pain

The brain cracked open
Migrainous in its attack

The psyche
no longer able
to straddle the two worlds

The dysfunction
Contouring the surroundings
Breeding toad medicine
Frogs for protection
Against the stain of the mother
A phobia
Keeping a distance
from a hedonist rage

The feral unleashing of awakening
begins to lessen its roar
The volume idles
into the tepid resignation of responsibility

The wound of the mother
Leaves the child alone
to cover the stench of sickness

ABANDON

The thin red line
stretched
beyond capacity

The child left
void of mother's touch

Abandoned to Spirit
To Divine Mother
to harbor her soul

Tiny paper thin cuts
derailed
by pinpricks of hope

Until the final slash
severs the arm

The crime scene
doused in alcohol
addiction

Flecks of blood still stain the walls
The memory remains

The heart recoiled
hope tainted
invest elsewhere

In the father

Ill but present
Never to abandon
to devote
dedicate
sacrifice
In hemorrhagic attire
his wellbeing
becomes the survival fracture

Anxiety attachment is born
the twists
of loss
entwine
with the dreaded turns
of terror

Both wounds
bleed
pulling the sutures
in opposition

Taut rigidity
Stress becomes the perfumed aroma

A war chest
encrusts the heart

Never abandon
Never commit elsewhere

Martyr the cause
Profit from isolation

Other families bleed into adoption
The orphan is on the loose

Intimacy worships
the protective stance of isolation

Distance becomes the creed
Independence sanctions survival

Yet in the loins
A child cries for love
A parental touch of safety
of protection
of tenderness

Not stained
with a predator's stench

The prey lands
Talons squared
A bird's eye view
of emotional distancing

Tender morsels of giving
Strips of flesh
lost in the squander of sacrifice

All lay fallow
in this hallowed ground

WILDLING

Rough
Wild
Untamed around the edges

Left to run feral
A power scourging the skin
A life force trapped beneath the crown
Born of spirit
Evoked by nature
Provoked by neglect

An urchin left on dry land
The firefly trapped in the jar of a body
The snake recoils her fangs
The dancing becomes still
The throat caves inward to be silenced

The power ignites once in a blue while
Shakti awakening its stance
Through pain
Through loss
Through the heartbreak of cruelty

Sexual domination over a child
The wielding of violence over a child
The tying to the bed of a child

These constraints
Trap the power in the genie's bottle
of its own making

Numbed by substances
Numbed by invocation to serve
Numbed by responsibility
Stifled by the fierce stronghold
Life left unsafe to receive

Not allowing softness too close
Keeping love at bay

Tightening the grip
The vessel remains airtight
A sealed protectant
A stance where survival wields its own sword

Until a birthright is claimed
Druid by nature
Magi circling in the cells
Awakening claims its own becoming
A whispered beckoning

Go against the self
The history
The thoughts

Until freedom once again
claims her breath

SACRIFICIAL LAMB

A mighty warrior
Fierce
Sacrificing for the cause

Trained in battle
A seer of the future
A keeper of the past

Her holy grail to champion her loved ones
To save them
To prove her loyalty
Her love

Fueled by the sacrificial mother
A lack of belief in her worth

When love and value are inextricably bound
Never enough to just be
Living in tainted waters
Fierce to prove her worthiness
her importance
her value

Always deemed in the eyes of another
Dangerous ground when the mirror's reflection
is shattered by their own demons

In the dead of night
she leaves to fight unseen threats
For those she cherishes
Her tribe

And fight she did
Returning triumphant in heart
Yet bloody and broken to the bone
Her army of organs hemorrhaging beyond belief
Legions of exhaustion lie wasted on the earth

To return home
No accolades
No caring

They did not see
They did not even know she had fought the conflict
Never understood why she betrayed herself

No appreciation
No love in return
No worth to be found

No one came
to bathe her weeping
bloody
wounds

The battle won
at a mighty cost

Yet the squalor of a war built on lack of worth
Abandoned to the hands of another
Always serving another master

rages on

THREE STRIKES

Strike one
A child
left to fend for the unwell father
The keen eagle eye of survival knowing
He must stay alive so foster care
is not the last resort

A family broken into shards
At least this the devil you know
The commitment made
Little fists clenched in white knuckles
The immature tongue sharpened
Keep him alive the mantra

A tiny frame parenting the giant of a man
Sitting over dinners of jarred pickles
A fierce
codependent protective stance
envelops
sucking out her breath

The child in bed
The phone echoes in the hallway
She wanders with sleep in her eyes to answer
This not usually her job

They ask for her father
she looks
she calls

A cavernous silence responds
No one is home

Fear steals her breath
The tragedy
not fear for herself being alone
but the fear her father is gone
Months before the mother had left
and not returned

The tiny frame crawls back into bed
Even the dog has gone
The house silent and still
Muted dreaded prayers for daylight to come
As fetal position becomes the only recourse

The father returns early
Uncomfortable in being caught away
Spending the night with his lover
Leaving his child alone

The psyche of this child
Now tormented by lack of trust
Contorted with the anxious need
to still keep him alive

How to keep him unharmed
if she cannot find him
is now the conflict that cracks her brain in two

Strike two
Time passes
The child told by the father
I cannot take care of you
Even though vicious battles
were fought in courtrooms
until full custody was won

A uniform bought
Name tags sewn

A child's body dressed in dark brown
Dropped at the dustbin gate of a boarding school

The father walks away
No contact for six weeks
There is a hunch to his body
Maybe his heart is breaking too

A child nine years of age
Already shattered by abandonment
by addiction
by abuse and neglect

Betrayal sears the heart
A trunk of no belongings becomes the only territory
Nothing personal allowed
All innocence left
The reek of rejection already smoldering
its fire now doused with gasoline

This is no Harry Potter
Even if the school is named Wychwood
The Dragon school down the road

The fetal position recalled
A horsehair mattress on a wired bed
Fed prison food
A hot water bottle battles against the cold
The only comfort for chilblained fingers and toes

Loss of all familiar
Silent tears weep under the bed covers
The English creed of stiff upper lip
Devoid of emotion
This religion hailed from the rooftops

A culture normalizing child abuse
enslaved to this monastic barbaric doctrine

Again the searing scream silently in the head
How can I keep the father safe
if I cannot be there for him
A new dread erupts
This prison is now home

Strike three
In time
visit home allowed
A new house
This woman
A new family

New brothers
The eye catches a small box by the front door
A card written in the father's scrawl
To the woman
With all my love

Stomach punches inward
The heart recoils

The psyche of a child
Unconditional love unknown
Fathomless love undiscovered
in this world of survival
Love is limited
Safety is unstable
If all his love is for her...

In disbelief the child soldier sent back to school
Now knowing this is for keeps
Captive in the system

A felony of torment is born
The imprisonment of the wounds begins

THE LAST MILE

The policemen at the door
Awkward
Guilt in their eyes

I am sorry, he begins
we cannot keep coming here to help
My father lies bleeding on the floor
Two strong men hauling him under the armpits
back into his wheelchair
The look of pity
bestowed on me as they leave

A moment sliced by clarity
This, whatever this is
is no longer sustainable

As I wheel him to his bed
With no dignity left
get him undressed
catheter in hand
His anger seething through every cell of his body
Betrayed
disheveled
dying from the inside out

I know in this piercing
I can no longer bear this burden
I can no longer take decent care or help this man

My father
dissolving before my eyes

Such decisions to make
Such battles to win

The conversation
dies a death before it begins
His answer a resounding no
He will not go into a home

My heart breaks in knowing
I have to override
the last sliver of his dignity
left in his disabled life
His hallucination of independence

Quietly behind the scenes
I find a home
for the young
for the disabled
for the dying

It is on a river
one of his loves
It is small
he would have his own room
With hoists
disabled showers
oxygen
everything

a bag of bones
needs to stay alive

The caveat
someone needs to die
to give up a space

The way forward
a wish for a death
To prolong a dying man's torture

The other caveat
as if more than one is ever needed
These homes are expensive

So in a web of lies
deceit begins
Working behind the fray

Without a clue
a seventeen year old daughter
Writes letters
Pleads
begs
weeps
Arrives on doorsteps
of strangers
of social workers

Visits the home
to decide who might die first

His home
his sanctuary
his hope
is put up for sale
to afford his new prison

All in secrecy
To evoke a sense of security
The lie begets such lies

A farm is found for his dog
waiting
silently
for death's call

His name not first on the list
Yet angels of compassion were at work
seeing this daughter
unable to care
unable to sustain
unable to lift
a dying father
anymore

The tables turn
The child now the parent
no longer willing to argue
or listen
or negotiate

You are moving to this home
Because you have to
Because I said so
Because I cannot take care of you anymore

Both hearts break

Even the name reeks of fraud
The place has a stench
of urine
of decay
A waiting room for death

This is not a home
It is not a sanctuary
It is simply a foyer for the end

The final drive to leave him there
The heartbreak losing his dog
The return to the flat to pack it up
The trips to storage
The money deposited to pay for this death march

So much done alone
Tracks in the brain
Associating stress and trauma
Adulting on steroids

For this
his last mile

DEATH WALKS BEFORE ME

Years in waiting
The death march finally beating its drum
An echo tilts the quieting of the breath
The death rattle pierces the silence
The space between the breath
becomes unbearable in length

The daughter
Her 21st birthday
Sits bedside
In prayer
Holding the skeletal hand
All but gone this father of hers
Yet a torrid shaky breath
still rattles the air

She holds her breath
in between the exhaustive silence
Again and again believing him dead
Again and again a fledgling rasp
quivers from his lungs

How is it possible
This bag of bones
Draped in skin
Everything lost
yet still alive

The will to live if organs still able
Heartrendingly unbelievable

Close to the midnight hour
The last breath drains from his decayed body
Silence finally falls
Filling the room
Piercing her heart
Time and space stand still in this honoring of death

Now an orphan to this man
Her life purpose
Her responsibility complete
His birthday gift to her
freedom

The gentle hand of the Irish
Embodied in a young man
A caregiver
Adored by the father

Takes her hand
Walks her from the fetal position of death
A chair is offered
in the quiet stainless steel of a kitchen
A glass of whiskey handed
The bottle taken

Time immemorial
A return to his room

His body laid out
All six feet four of majestic frame
In years
never witnessing the full stretch of his grandeur

Finally he looks at peace

Death walked by
to return this soul home

A PROTECTION STANCE

A calling to explore kibbutz life
A hope of community
A desire to live off the land

Within weeks the cotton fields sold
in trade for shares in a plastics factory

Affairs
Gossip
Dissatisfaction
Woven throughout a spirited survival
of togetherness

Head shaved
Army uniform adorned
Soldier boyfriend found
All to keep the lechery at bay

Yet there were pearls in the swine

A man named Natty
Stood high above the rest
Bearded in wisdom
Eyes pooled in kindness
A sage in human clothing

He saw a light in this young being
A need for initiation

A desire for integration

The guardian he became
An angel of guidance
An alliance to adulthood
no one else had afforded

The horses their common ground
Paper making their meditation
His fierce protection
a salve for all who had failed
or taken advantage before

Twelve Israeli men
A tradition on horseback for days in the desert
Sleeping nights with the Bedouins
The desert dwellers in their hallowed tents

She was invited
A woman never gone before
Natty held his ground as elder
The other alphas angry
This breaking of the creed

Her horse pregnant
Their connection deep
Her work to care for these beasts of beauty

She was warned
These men are wolves

Protect yourself
The lesson begins under guidance foretold

Ecstasy
Thirteen horses
galloping along the Jordanian border
Lightning strikes
Thunder roars
The same defiance rising in these men

Riding hours through shingle
Cliff edges slide to nowhere
She dismounts her pregnant belly
Helps
hauls
guides her footing so the three of them survive

At night
The only female
Lying down in blackened tents
Hookah smoke fills the air

With men
With desert gypsies
With horses
Strangely safe
She is a curiosity no less

Day after day
The burden of proof

With Natty's protective eye
Without him
knowing she would be prey

The men finally realize
She can take care of herself
She can ride as them
She can sleep on rock with them
She can drink with them
She becomes one of them

An initiation into womanhood
into equality
into capacity
into the piercing of Natty's shielding presence

Forever grateful
His care provoked the birthing
of this protection stance
Never displayed
Never given before
Penetrates
A sanctuary deep in her own being

In time the foal birthed
A new beginning of life
Legs wobbly
Same shelter needed
Given her namesake
Miranda

A memory
A gifted legacy
to be lived on

A BLOOD RED PILGRIMAGE

Where sapphire waters
brim desert sands
Desert dwellers
Draped in robes
live on this earth

Bedouins
A tribe of ancients

A backdrop of mountains
Surround the harsh environment

Bodies and minds adaptive
in archaic ways of survival
Basked in tradition

Women wrapped in black
Head to foot
No curve allowed
The burqa conceals all form

On each day
a gathering goes walkabout
Alone
these silent women
set foot towards barren rocks
until the silhouettes
become dusk

Disappearing ghostlike
into treacherous terrain

A curiosity
These women
Where are they going

Into a cavernous emptiness
Seemingly with nothing to offer

The question asked
A Bedouin friend
Enough English to talk camel
What of this journey of women

They are bleeding
They are unclean
Not able to touch food
So they travel to the mountain
To bleed together on harsh lands

A few days without responsibility
A hooded peak
A blackened tent
A haven for the red blood

Women together
A sisterhood of menses
Resting
Squatting

For a season
free of ownership

This time spent living in Egypt
Treacherous truths revealed
The reason patriarchal in horror
A corruption of the feminine
Disfiguring sexuality
In ways
that twist the mind
break the heart
sicken the stomach

Yet this female pilgrimage
The reason harrowing
The result
a pause in life
a moment to go inward
to thaw

A sacrifice
A wavering to make sacred
The sloughing of the uterus
The inner sanctum allowed to rest
The desire to be alone revered
The cycle of womanhood
A death before birth

Sanctioned
Made holy
Respected

The feminine altar most high
The flowing of the body

The feminine unadulterated
by the masculine
A cherishing of menstruation
Faithful in the ways of nature

To the internal scream
casting off the past
The compass reset
To halt the incessant demands

The suffocating partnership
between colonized society
in bed with civilized insanity

To ignore the undulation of female creativity
To pretend the shedding of blood does not exist
Does not need to be honored
Left tainted
Stained in masculine conditioning

Disbelieve these incantations
Release the spell
Unravel the matrix

Meet your bleeding with reverence
Embrace the hormones on fire
Listen intently to the banshee wail of truth
of all that is being ignored

No longer follow the patriarchal destiny
The shackled imprisonment
of a woman's
sacred
blood
falling
from
her
body

ORPHANS OF LIGHT

Who have we become
two orphans of light

When love expressed
through a clenched jaw
on fire with rage

When care
recklessly displayed
with an iron fist
and a jagged tongue

When attachment
met with neglect
Anxiety provoking
Confusion reigns

When a child births a child
Mothering twists its fate
into resentment and steel

The ground of existence
becomes a realm of terror
The infant left in the cold ice
of emotional disconnect

When neglect is the creed
The mother's heart echoes
the emptiness in the womb

Fertile for life
Barren for love

What have we become
Two children of abuse

Now grown into mothers
in our own being

Cousins
With mothers broken
from the same ancestry

Yet by some miracle
This did not break
these motherless souls

Instead the capacity grew
in the resilience of love

To forgive
To care
To tend to
Karmic rewards indeed

Both lights rose from the ashes
Between the cast iron shards of careless parenting
They soared on broken wing
above the destruction

To find love in their hearts
Even if the responsibility
still has the stench
of the broken mother

This light unprotected
Unshielded from predators
who live in their own shadows
Who are hollow banshees for the shining

A capacity to sustain character
Through the slivered veils of trauma

Two orphans of light continue to shine

IN BETWEEN WORLDS

A sacred anointing
With heart
face
intent
turned towards the seat of the guru

The back turned to the past
dissolving relics into the truth itself

A receiving of the known and the unknown
An anointment in the divine
A return to the womb of Divine Mother

A remembering
The true nature and essence
before all was forgotten
by thought
ignorance
conditioning

The knots disentangled
Dissolving the shadow for the light to shine through

Mourning the delusion
The fortress of separation
Mastering the knowledge
In reverence to the lineage alive in the succession

A return home

Lessons learned
Spiritual knowledge imparted
Teachings integrated
An actualization of all that is pure

Such the gifts from the sages
From those who have gone before
For those who will walk ahead
Shakti transmitted heart to heart
The eyes of the teacher brimming
with awakened light
Pierces the doorway to the soul of the seeker

Mala beads blessed
gifted
Laid with love around the shoulders
Encircling the heart
Embodied with awakening

The journey ends here
The journey begins here
The guru is birthed within

Meditation the commitment
Practice the compass
Discipline the devotion
Kindness the creed

Establishing a divine presence here on earth
Accomplishing a divine mission here on earth
Integrating divinity here on earth

As Shakti
now embodied
walks a new earth

THE PROPOSAL

A simple plan
To survive
Yet commit to awakening into the realms of spirit

Marry God and all will be made in heaven
as I openheartedly said I do

An escape from dysfunction
From the slavery of the bloody constellation
which I call family

Engaged with spirit
yet still tethered by guilt and responsibility
Holding the knife's edge for the bloodline
in fear of their lives
Their actions of self destruction

As I honeymooned in heaven
I enslaved others to ground my hell on earth

Proposal after proposal refused
in desperation
to control the square edges of existence

Yet slowly
Surely it began
An opening to supreme emptiness
An awakening

Making absolutely no sense at all
As the opening opened
The awakened awakened
The enlightenment ignited

So too did all the areas of the managed life
so neatly and efficiently tied down

It seems when you wake up
so do the sleeping dragons
The sharp edges of veiled delusions
A pilgrimage to the mass forgotten graves
The embodied realms of hell
The chill winds of reality

Limited beliefs no longer hold sway
The ground now moving beneath my feet

Swift rapids pour forth all that was closed
The debris of relationships
The mantles of fear
The raw nerve of vulnerability exposed

A torrent of all that had been resisted
All I had refused

Basking in the tender shoots of enlightenment
A laugh peals forth from the irony of beliefs
The delusion I could choose what I would awaken to

Hilarious really
If you turn on the light
It lights the whole room
The tide rises
so do all ships

And now I am married
A long term marriage
to all I had devotedly divorced

Awakening

Remembering

The simple paradox of ascension

Leaving me deeper
in the trenches of life
than ever before

BLOOD IN THE WATERS

To lie in the arms
of what seems love

To be beckoned
by charms
deception
promotion

Seduced by the intense moments of connection

Only to be starved in the wasteland
until the next drop of rain
drenches the parched heart

The game of cat and mouse has begun
yet not knowing you are the mouse
or there is even a cat

To be the mark
as the gypsies would say

To be prey to a beast
without conscience

To be fodder for the one
who is always emptied

Whose insatiable appetite
is to devour what is you

The more powerful
The more brilliant
The more light
The more attractive

The more
you become the food
to the feeding frenzy of the sociopath

The more you open your heart
the more you give
the more they take

Isolating you from those you love
Turning twisted events
Well intentioned words
into bloodstained matter

A deep internal voice stirs
A warning
yet this reluctance ignored
The trusting innocent heart
unprepared for the onslaught

Pathological lying
Ruthless selfishness

Merciless blame
All corrode away at your worth

A separation so fierce
The only desire for its own saturation of needs

Parasite in human form
Tentacles wrapped around your heart

Strangling the mind
Suffocating the body
sucking
pulsing
bleeding

Leeches on fire
burrowing deep
Raped of it all
The angel doing the devil's bidding

Until without breath left in the body
No marrow left in the bones

Emptied of life force
of money
of worth

With nothing left to give

The sociopath takes its last lick
and walks away

In search of new prey

Leaving you a shell
A memory of the fierce light you once were

Every ounce of your character stretched
torn
tattered
unraveled to its edge

Frayed in the occultist desire
to understand behavior beyond your nature

Every cell in the body
Torqued further than its limit
Yet in this stench of death a new horizon is born

A knowing
A wisdom
An intuition
which smells the sociopath as it walks into the room
Once abused
The victim can always sense the predator

In this cathartic remembering
An awakening
you are reborn
as your true nature

The threadbare shreds of life
are called back home

to a conversation
deep within yourself

A communion of knowing your worth
once destroyed
An intimacy with values no longer threatened

A solid ground of being
Restoring the most precious of relationships
with the self

Worthy of protection
Now choosing who to call in close

The inner circle
of business
in partnership
in love

Discernment
born of experience

A bird's eye view
of understanding human nature

The ruthlessness of the sociopath
Chilling the bones with no remorse
Drenches world history

The light in the shadow
No longer drowning in anguish

A legacy is built
Those without care
forever uninvited
left at the door

With the deep resonant
orchestral bellow
a boundary of NO

A reckoning with reality
Acknowledging
Recognizing
all the sociopaths who live next door

Yet
forever grateful
for this diabolical lesson

SCORPIO NATURE

On this day
A remembrance of time gone by
An embryo
unleashing her Shakti onto this world

A spark of life
Born of love
Fluttering in the belly of the womb

Rising from the ashes
of lifetimes past
A profound yes to potentize life

A call and response
For life to remember
For breath to breathe
For creation to create

What is birthing
under the eaves of unconsciousness

Fifty years in the making
Ever widening circles
A ripple across the universe
A footprint left in the sand
The tides ever changing
Leaving no stone unturned

Do not grieve for the wilting of what was
The moon does not sadden her waning

Stoke the fire
The longing
This yearning for life
A call to service

Destroy the résumé
Declare the virtues of the eulogy

A rhapsody
A bohemian symphony
Whispering your name

An old soul
with gypsy blood
Magi in her bones

Lay waste to what was
Burn the torrid stories
Tear them to the ground

The myth of separation
The darkness of fear
The shameful tirade of overwhelm

Untangle the knots
The thread of limitation

The shackles of society
The ropes of conformity

Unravel
Reveal
Bestow beauty in her wake
Unite in compassion
Revel in generosity
Awaken to consciousness

Become a Celtic beauty
A knot of amazing grace
Intertwined
Interconnected

Oneness
Woven
Weaved
Waxed
Waned

In this space
This presence
This emptiness

What is awakening
Birthing
What is tender within
Vulnerable to the touch

What is stirring
Rising
Growing
Yearning
Desiring
Unfolding

What is drenched in creation
Praying for release to be unfurled

Let her be free
Unleashed from traditions

The seed is stirring
Cracking open her husk to be stunned by life

This potent power of simply being
Nourish the embodiment
Animate what is tender
embryonic
growing within you

LET US ANOINT THIS HOME

A yes
Fell out of me
Ten years before
Agreed in innocence

The tide
pulled
on a wave
pouring the current forward
in unseen directions

To grow
To expand
Drowning
in responsibility

A bite too large
Indigestible

A marriage
to bricks
to mortar
to duty

Home
Shelter
Adorned
Anointed in spirit

Pouring forth
Overflowing
with minutiae

The body expands
in a torrid attempt
to hold the burden

Rain pours
Deadening the weight
Dragging the mass home
Tears roll down
stained cheeks

A look to heaven
A single cry
This is too big for one person

The choice
to dismantle the shingles

Each seed
grows roots
tearing at the earth
cracking at the seams

I offer you up
Dear surrender
I offer you to another
Back to where you belong

I pray you are cherished
Nurtured

Deep pockets
to lay you waste

To pour new love
new vision
into your bones

I offer you back
The gentle stream

A sanctuary
to many

This land
A refuge
An asylum

Family
Home
Attunements
Silence
Retreats
Tears
Laughter
Transformation
Healing for us all

A haven
polarized
with debt
with investment
with profit

Ley lines
turn their course

I implore
for freedom

The way forward
a Docusign extravaganza

I release you
With my love
With my deepest gratitude

For your shelter
Your beauty

Dearly
beloved
home

UNAVAILABLE

Like a moth to a flame
An air of unavailability hangs in the air
Smoke from a cigarette
waiting for the gentlest breeze
to disintegrate its form

The more elusive
The more unavailable
The greater the attraction

A familiar bond of neglect feeds this frenzy
The wound wretched for a mother's love
On the hunt to salvage
the wreckage of the past
Same energy
yet desperate for a different result

The definition of insanity

The traction addictive
The less accessible
The greater the need

The circus begins

Costumed in self reliance
Egoic manipulations arise

Pleading for the love
hollowed in the empty cave of the heart

The caveat
The familiar abandonment wound

Partnered with the father's love
Tortured in codependency because of illness
Leaves the psyche shattered
into shards of intimate love
Falling strewn on the floor
Drenched in pools of blood

Desperate hands
gather the carnage
Held to the bleeding heart
in rivers of tears

The same funeral pyre
marches on
A keening heartbreak
rattles the night air

If unavailability is the choice
By an unconscious design now made aware

The casket is already made
The lid always ajar
The relationship destined before it began

To lay its decaying body of flesh
in the plush velvet of death

Yet an invitation offered
A different dance party
Instead of chasing the dragon
The junkie's harrowing storyline

A team of safe support
offers loving hands

To bear witness
to stay close
to not leave

In this gift
In this consciousness
the healing made clear

To no longer abandon the self
To be available to the pain body
To heal the wound
rather than reenact it

To no longer betray
To live with the abandon of choosing the self
The heart full
Worth buoyant
Self respect resilient

To choose such a love
A resplendent love

Available
Vulnerable
A mirror
of what is now birthing
on the inside

AN ALCHEMY OF GRACE AND HELL

When the body
Betrayed by actions
Exiled from life force
Left to live in the dark
Shadowed in lost integrity

Responds in kind

The distortion grows
A bindweed strangles harmony

The bones
the tissue
the flesh
deforms the surface below

Time takes its toll
The thoughts destroy
The habits decay
The fractured energy finally manifest
Disease is born

Once density has a strong hold
Carved in the steel mechanics of form
A knife blade becomes the only option

Drips of anesthesia
A temporary grave invoked

Vital for the action
For the execution of the surgeon's hand
Steel swords
Stitches woven
Tattered scars tattooed

A literal death state
So the surgeon's scalpel
with precision
can cut deep
and wide
Splaying open the tender flesh

Where the external world
meets the internal world
Without the boundaries
of skin
muscle
sheaths
Function can no longer reside

Blunt force trauma
meets tender flesh

Organs retract, handled by metal hands
A sterile environment drowns life force

A freeze occurs
Survival howls silently
from the edges of consciousness

As a death march moves across the body

In this state of dying
A miracle occurs
Organs moved
Flesh stitched
Blood infused
Oxygen breathed
Drugs given

This battlefield
a war zone
only crossed
out of desperation

Forces at play
into the hands
of utter surrender

The surgeon's last words
You need to trust me

Fear forced to dissolve into trust
The miracle of the body under siege
The wonder of awakening
The primal instinct of the body
Righting itself back to health

The wounded animal awakens
from the deepest of slumber

Hunched
Turned inward
Unable to run or protect
however much life depends on it
Vulnerability seared into humanity

Love and care abound
The injured body unable to fend for itself

A village of angels
Devote love into the cracks
of this surgical wasteland
Patiently
Lovingly
until vitality also regains consciousness

The deed is done
A walk towards the knife was chosen
Deepest gratitude abounds
in this alchemy of grace and hell

ALCHEMICAL

A year without silence
A year without retreat
The pandemic forced agitation in all of the cracks
The hidden crevices of the psyche

The character already born
stretched to the limit of endurance
Capacity vanquished
Resilience drained
The stress fracture inflames values
drenched in the prolonged agony of the unknown

Fear caught fire by relentless change
Adaptability fraught with survival
until the fists of fundamentalism rise up
red hot above the fray

A sanctuary needed
A release yearned for
A safe haven
To funnel
to allow
to explore
to heal the parts this trauma triggered
by a death threat
by isolation
by loss of contact

An offering made
Toad medicine
A spirit animal from the past
Three days in ceremony
Three days in silence
Three days in medicine
Three days in prayer
The pilgrimage to go inward
To go quiet
To receive

The well filled
The fractures in the foundation restored
All that gravity held close
loosened its grip

A liberation released
Unconditional love honored
The sovereignty of the ancestors claimed
What was needed given

A gift from spirit
A gift of grace
A gift of love

Forged on a bedrock of gratitude

A COMMUNION

Prayers birth
a communion with spirit

Firewater in the eye
Burning its path to the third eye
Tobacco and herbs snuffed
Cracking the heart open
with startling intensity

A glass pipe
Meth-like in its horror
The toad medicine
Small crystals
lying fallow in the glass dome

Permission is asked
Permission is granted
The pipe held to the heart
Intention set
In deepest gratitude
to Sapito
The fire melts the poison
Smoke fills the bowl

Instructions clear
Smooth slow inhale

The alchemy
from poison to medicine
A sharpness
fills the lungs
The breath held

More medicine offered
More taken

And in an instant
The world implodes
Energy courses up
through the chakras
Exploding at the third eye
The surrender fathomless
A fall from the cliff edge
Instantaneous in its direction
Relentless in its collapse of form

A new plateau is built
A laser light penetrates the brain
Burrowing deep
The craggy edges melted
into the light of spirit

More medicine offered
A hand goes up
Clear
direct
in a strong no

The surge of energy
Annihilates all external senses
The eyes fall inward
The breath taken

A momentary death state
Collides with the world all as one
The body falls back to the earth
Unable to hold structure

She writhes
Snakelike
as the energy
courses the systems of the body

Beings in form
Many in spirit
Circle
with heartbeats
Feathers
Drum beats
Smoke
Prayers
Ancient song
Roses
Fragrance

A call to the ancestors
The body rises back up

Hands claw the earth
Desperate for grounding

The eyes lock
The healer meets the healer
The wounded child meets Ma
The weeping of grief racks the body
The snake of suffering
coiling and recoiling
in desperation for escape

Such a container
of unconditional love held

Grief for the child
Tears for the mass consciousness of sorrow

Questions asked
Who is this ancestor?
Calling for recognition
Calling her way home

She is light
She is not of this earth
Her energy broke countless grandmothers
Yet now meeting
She is home
as the two energies
reside as one

A relief at the embodiment
A grace as the ancestors are healed
Integration at last

The energy slows
Moments of such stillness
No need to breathe
as prana courses through the veins

Fire is offered
An eternal flame
Hands and energy play
as torment is given back to spirit

Tobacco is asked for
Cacao given
Hot tea cradled

The breath returns
The room returns
The circle of women present

Ceremony has begun

UNCHARTED TERRITORY

The devil rises
as firewater along the urinary tract

Dehydration plays a part
Intimacy also
yet deep at the root
terror is the cause

When sexuality begins as a child
A part taken by the predator
that which never belonged to them

Purity lost
dissolved into a splintered soul
Stolen by another's distorted lust to devour
Their sin becomes the abused cross to bear
The internal territory of the body
no longer her own
protected
safe

In the body of a child
only innocence was stirring
Yet now an experience awakened
unable to go back to sleep
Wonder shattered
The sanctity of shelter
never to return

Not on her terms
No boundaries learnt
No body ready

The edges of the psyche cracked open
Torn into tatters
Unbearable in harrowing ways
A scar tissue of resilience
A tolerance for the crimes of another is born
No room to develop
sacred intimacy
harbors of safety

A crash landing of maturity
A void encrusts any doorways
to healthy loving partnership
Sensuality no longer unearthed
Forever unseeded in virtue

Sexuality becomes a tool
A lethal weapon others wield
The pendulum swings
Feeling desired translates into distortions of love
Stapled together with fear

The child unable to set a tethering
to her birthright of boundaries

The last encounter
with a beast of prey

Years too many
spent with a shamanic sociopath

A predator energy
Familiar
A vampire she invited in
Devouring her body again and again
Insatiable in its appetite
Attraction turned to disgust
Her internal voice screaming
yet the silence remained

The trauma from childhood provoked
by discernment's extinction

Until with a crescendo of grace
the universe conspired
to end what was destroying her

Betrayals
Deceit beyond belief
Finally the addiction to the distortion of love
The fiery attachment to the wound gone rogue
dissolved enough to walk away

Ten years healing
Ten years in celibacy
Ten years in love
An old flame across an ocean
safe in the distance

Until the day came
when love cracked opened the door
A love of such respect
Connection
Care

For this invitation to be honored
a healing must occur
A reconciliation deep below the conscious mind
in the bowels of dread

Rectifying the belief
she is not safe in her own dominion
Resilience in becoming her own advocate
Building the capacity to set boundaries
The courage to speak truth
The revelation that sex does not equal love
Sex does not make the abandoner stay
These the medicinal tinctures taken

This and more taken to ceremony
To call herself back
All the lost parts of her soul

The fear of no territory
Primal in its need to mark with urine
that which was never protected before

The UTI the messenger
Meeting fear in the eye

The guidance to go deep
To go wide
Vast beyond the territory of the story
Farther than the cellular memory of the experience

Back to the truth of sanctuary
residing within the body
Sheltered in the bedrock of the self
Never to abandon the authority of her own domain

This becomes the creed
The commitment
Wholeheartedly
to protect the part so afraid

To meet sexuality as a woman
Intercourse as communion
A conversation of intimate proportion

Respect at the helm
In power
In advocacy

At last
the risk of vulnerability
caressed
in the refuge
of a tenderhearted embrace

A COLLISION OF PAST AND FUTURE

News of a birth bubbles up with delight
The heart breaks into shattered pieces of expansion
A new life conceived in the purest of love

In the expectant eyes of the grandmother
The daughter shifts on her axis
The kaleidoscope quivers
Young woman becomes mother
Life beckons deep within the womb

A joy exceeds capacity
Her partner becomes family
The son she always longed for
A union of ancestral bloodlines

This new beloved spark of life
Chosen into a family of such beauty
Of care
Respect
Loyalty

A decency lives at the core
A partnership of courage
Of vulnerable commitment

This terrain becomes the genesis
for this child to lie within
To enter this world into loving arms

Welcomed by so many

Yet a stirring ache collides with such rapture
Tentacles buried deep within the unconscious
Swaddled in years of healing
Yet still fragile
buried deep
in tombs of pain
An opportunity for deeper transformation
The ten thousand paper-thin cuts
Scribed on an ancient bleeding heart
unfurl with a quaking desire to rejoice

The oath shattered many moons before
To mother differently
The spell bound curse
broken for the mothers
Grandmothers
gone before

This matriarch to be
Remembering her own journey
back into the light
Her pregnancy
Her daughter
An angel in form
Provoked the broken limbs of hurt to heal
The desire to live
To embody with care
To cause no harm

To return the bleeding wounds
back to their own sullied conception
of the ancestors gone before

Years in the making
Determined to parent her daughter well
The wounded child birthed into mother
Committed to the harrowed uprising of healing
With heartfelt gratitude
to witness this new life unfolding
The torrid lineage made whole

This new generation
A beloved babe
born into cradling arms
hearts of wisdom
realms of love
A new father
A young mother
of exceptional
extraordinary values

As inception takes flight
Bestowed from divine grace
The miracle of creation enters this world

As the double-edged knife blade cuts deep
The polarized spectrums collide
Hope strikes trauma
Love shatters fear

The torch of light
passed on without all the shadow

This tender heart of trauma met with such care
A loving witness
pours wisdom
clarity
light
into this pool of darkness

Allowing the radiant luminosity
of even more love to birth

SACRED DOMINION

A connection
Destined to be found
Divine Mother places her hand
after years of devotion
Kindred intimacy

A communion born in sacred hallowed ground
Respect
Vulnerability
Such transmission
Bound in prayer
Steeped in silence
Set free by love

A love beyond the ages
A union unspoken
Patience in waiting
Journeys
rivers
mountains
to cross

Until freedom maps the course
Nothing in its way
Even distance has no claim

The energies unite
Defying space and time

Heart strung
Tapestries woven
Threads of humanity
cross thresholds
into the tender realms
of infinite
unconditional
love

"There are only two mistakes one can make
along the road to truth;
not going all the way
and not starting."
~ Buddha

KNOW WHO YOU TRULY ARE

Abide in the gravitational pull of truth

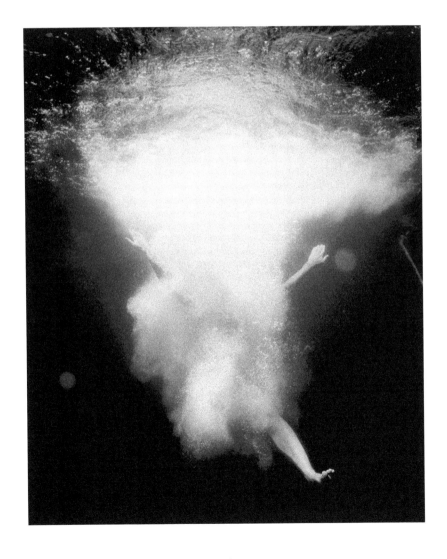

HUMAN ANIMAL

Discipline
sourced by steel

Folded in on itself
to pierce back into the flesh

Fueled by human animal
Tattooed in shoulds

Dutiful demands
Shrouding
the still quiet hum
of a soul's longing
to create
to dream
to draw
outside the lines

A heartbeat's
rhythmical rendering of desire

Lamenting its loss
as the mundane drowns the pulse

The oxygen
inhaled by tasks of protection
by demands of survival
The banshee wail for freedom

This
is where the metal
rips the road

Human necessity goes guttural
Steeped in confines
Drenched in heritage
Culture
Patriarchy

If left unattended
the tender light of spirit will drown
Tethered in the weight of iron shackles
In the embodiment of fear
Not always a good adviser

Devoured by obligation
Yet
if left unscathed
the heartbeat of creation will fuel a fire

So bright
as to burn
all conflict
all agita
to the ground

To illuminate
the guttural truth
of spirit

Whose innate power
is her heart cry

Always
and forever

Disobedient to suppression

THE CULLING

The wound
Seductive by nature

Provocative
Shiny in smoke and mirrors

Birthed in trauma
Fraught in delusion's fight

An experience
Compelled
Flooded
Scarred
by stress hormones

Undigestible in size
Unsurmountable

A rabid beast
Unable to course through its veins
Straddle its back
Fly its course

This wound lies barren
Raped by life
Left bleeding
forlorn on bloodied knee

Shrapnel left afloat
Hungry for sustenance
Starved for position

The suffering
Raptures as a ravenous ghost

Haunting the halls
of mind
of memory
of cellular damage

Provoking stories
Dramas
Situations
to support the skeleton bones
to feed the gnawing teeth
to keep the empty hallows alive

The shell of the wound
infertile
unless fed by familiar cries

Given life by similar experience
Flourished by victims' messaging
Inflamed if left alone

The hurt vigilant
Stay awake

The provocateur
pacing
waiting
stalking
the vulnerable cracks
in the psyche's domain

Vampiric in nature
Sucking on delusion's blood
Stealing life force

Strict adherence
to force nonempirical history
into matter

To feed the injury
soiled in sepsis

Cutting its teeth
To capture
Then imprison
the fragile democracy
of the empty present

BROKEN WILL

When authority submits its will
on the broken back of a child

The horse brought to its knees
The master
cruel
untethered
broken

Authority becomes the enemy
Dogma the threat
An internal autonomy grows
Inflamed by survival
Arrogant out of fear

A cohesive rationale when laws make no sense
Yet a lack of trust
infiltrates the rules
The boundaries
that might ever help

A stubborn control becomes the doctrine
An independent spirit suffocated by isolation
A pioneer gone rogue

To trust
To surrender
Both concepts unmitigated in despair

Self reliance becomes the creed
Marking out posts
of entrepreneurial leadership
Decorating self sufficiency as religion

Until a day arises with the sun cresting the moon

A foreshadowing of truth
A collapse of dictatorship

Self resilience fails
in an utter torrent out of control

The story line screams the twisted plot

The punch line falls flat in an arena of empty seats

Despair returns finally to inquiry

Control relinquishes to surrender

Authority
finally
takes a bow

PREDATOR

When you are filled with the light of spirit
The predator who prowls the shadow
hunts this radiance
this integrity
An energy to devour

When darkness craves luminosity
unable to source its own magnificence
The innocence lost
incapable of defending
becomes the mark

In and over and after time
the shimmer dims out of survival
Shrouded by its own darkness of despair

A uniform of black
Layers of protection
An armoring of the feminine
Sexuality hidden from view

Seeking safety in isolation
The passion flower slowly dies on the vine

An internal drought of connection
Service becomes the creed
A career bound in protocol

The world fraught without boundaries
The flicker shrouded from sight
A heavily armored response
Tactical in approach

Until the dawn arises
A light of its own accord
orbits the flame of spirit
with care
with consideration
with love

The melting of the steel
becomes the alchemy for this union
Such radiance meets its own frequency
A release of dread
No need to protect
A raw vulnerability unfiltered by fear

Knowing
when the stars of light meet
Sourced from their own cohesion
There is nothing to devour
hunger
or thirst for

As already overflowing
Treasured in devotion
In awe

A love sourced by the Divine

STAND DOWN

When innocence is left unattended
An infant
not only unprotected
but infiltrated
hurt
violated

A layer of armor is born
Steel shells
Harsh returns
bleed out into the wound
choosing enemy after enemy

Safety
A kite spurned in the wind
Stability built on unearthed tunnels of pain
Neglect the lullaby

In this marshland of fear
a general is born
She is strong
She is ruthless
She bows to no one
She builds laws
walls
boundaries

Greater than her heart
Taller than her body
Wider than her hug

When life is too soft
She hardens

When vulnerability echoes
She recoils

When intimacy dances
she escalates more layers

Fat cells her army
Inflammation the cavalry
Isolation her snipers

Symptoms inflame
as heart openings
arise

Then on such a day
A shimmering of hope
Reveals a bended knee
as a swell of deep gratitude
arises
to this gladiator
this protector
this empress of domain

The one always constant
The one who never betrays
abandons
means to cause harm

Her quest is protection
Instinctual primal defense
Above all else
Keep the powder dry
away from tears of loss

The intention to always be the ally
A sisterhood against the enemy at the door

The martial law
Do not trust
Do not be vulnerable

Yet with gratitude beyond words
With deepest appreciation
With the utmost respect
With the acknowledgment of her sacrifice

I thank her for her service

I ask her
head bowed in respect
as she meets me with blood in her eyes

What do you need
warrior behind my back
sword always drawn
teeth always ready

To lay down this old way
born out of survival

To return to holy ground
To entrust

What do you need, dear one

What do you need

to stand down

STENCH OF VANILLA

Shut down
Crippled by
intoxicating numbness

Dull to the touch
Tasteless to the bone
A stench of vanilla
through and through

Passion lost
Annihilated
by the tendrils of fear
insecurities
anxiety

Joy's ashes burnt to the ground
Inspiration shackled in the mundane

A fire hose of horizontal sleeplessness
in a warfare of normalcy
Against the tide
of creation

Caught in the flood of dormancy
A parallel death trap of denial
Asleep in depression's delusion

Wedged under the ice surface
Suffocating life force
Frozen in time
Dousing the spark of existence

Yet mourn no more
Solace is beckoning
A riptide of design

Reach for the gold-drenched
wonder of awe
Let it fall
ripple
descend
into life's beige creases

Curse compassion's darkness
Light the dusk crossing the heart
Dip into the shadow darkening the way

Ascend
Descend

Reach
Fold
Embrace

The swirl of gold-leafed magenta
Diamond studding the middle way

No longer frozen in the midpoint
as milk churns to cream
Thickening in desire
Yearning forward

The golden skies fall through the floor
The molten earth rises to meet the heavens

Betwixt
Between
The middle path implodes
Encompassing all that was lost

Inflaming the capacity
to embrace it all

WILD WISDOM

Wild one
Seething beneath the surface
of confined behavior

Writhing snakelike
Fangs at the ready
to defend herself against
condemnation
judgment
more exile

Coiled in the corner
The farthest reaches
Caged from life's pleasures

The fear and dread
of granting her freedom

Her passion's desire
to rip the controlled stance apart

Left guarded heavily at the door
So as not to unleash her back onto the world

This feral beauty will risk it all
if left unbound

The bloodbath of her banshee cry
will echo across the horizon

If left untethered
Heralding the fire dragon
She will burn it all to the ground
A flame so bright as to reveal only truth

If unshackled
Shameless
She will fight
She will defy

Rebellious by nature
Enraged
Hurling
Erupting wide open
The wound gone sour

The gaping sore
of division
of separation

A life lived
Condemned by the critic
Religion
The patriarch
The afraid
The conformist
The need to be liked

The mother
whose eagle eye
holds with a steel grip
Shuts the heathen down
Restricts her latitude

The facade engulfs her
Layer upon layer
of who she is not

Afraid of the prophet's power
The might
the ability to smite
to destroy
to hurt

To pierce
deep in the eye
To ring
the toll bell of truth

Surrender taming this wild one
Renounce the control
Obey the genie within
The one who embodies such sovereignty

Stop the ravages of this war
Know she belongs

Embrace her storm

Her wisdom
Her faith

She who holds the freedom
The autonomy
The crusade

To walk tall
Head high
Free from judgment
Wild as hell

Release her domain
Her light
Her shadow

Yield to the blessing of her
The way of her
The spirit of her

Unravel the chaos
Loosen her bondage
Release the straitjacket

Feel her pulse
Her dance
Her heartbeat

Her footprint
The sway of her hips

Embrace her enchantment
Her wanton stare
Her desire to destroy and birth
All in the same moment

Love her
Cherish her
Set her free

Untame her wild heart
Be grateful for her valiant spirit

Be faithful to her
as she has always been to you

FURY BOUND

A dark heart
torn and tattered

Veils draped
over honor

A sin scars the essence of being
Possessed by fear or pain

Love left bleeding
without power to change the course

Blinded by all that was cherished
gone bad
hurt
betrayed
rejected

Hate echoes the war cry
as pain turns to this powerful ally
Betrayed by lack of choice
Contracts scrawled in blood

Retribution
Revenge
Cruelty

In the blink of an eye
suffocating
all that is good
kind
tender

There will be blood
As unconsciousness reigns
Such justification
led by temptation
The thrust of torment
Not enough daylight
The earthbound chatter possesses the mind
beyond a recall of decency

Entity driven
Fury bound

The shroud tightens
The denial strengthens its grip

Lost to an underworld of resentment
Hope shattered
Crushed as a fist
to a butterfly wing

What is this shadow laid over the soul
A silhouette of dusk vanquishes integrity

What lies heavy
pulling at the strings of the heart

A sin beyond memory
A betrayal to the bone
An action unthinkable

The crime committed
has becomes personal
in the hunger for punishment

Burdened
Begging for confession

The victim becomes the perpetrator
ravaging the soul

Reveal the judgment
Lay waste to what threatens
the whisper of decency

Emancipate yourself
Dismantle the meat hooks
attaching you to the external ache

Remember anger is simply
the top note of sorrow
Grief lays fallow beneath

Set yourself free

Grant forgiveness as the final step
on the ten thousand trodden
on freedom's path
Forgiveness of the other
Forgiveness of yourself

Make love to the loathing
Dissolve hate's arc of power
Declare the darkness back to light

MYTHOLOGY IN THE MAKING

A dread begins to build
Silent at first
Creeps its way in the doorway
Uninvited
Pouring around the edges into the psyche

A catastrophic feeling
A connection lost
of great importance

Out of reach
cracks the mold of security

Innocent in its origins
Yet the torrid belief
Deserving of punishment
You did something wrong
No logic allowed

The lost union
Airway silence
Haunted by the narrative
A word
An action
becomes the mythology
which breaks the back

A one-sided conversation begins
The mind on fire

Unbelievable horror stories written
Inked across the brain

Enters the body
Inflames the nervous system
Retraumatizes the flailing wound

Steals the breath
Shuts down the systems of coherence

The object of affection
unaware
Oblivious to the decision
the wounded child has reached

It is over
What was said destroyed
The strategy for you to love me
Shattered
Broken in one action
Too authentic
Too real

The reality tipped
The fragile tapestry keeping it alive
The tiny thread of oxygen in the room
lost in one foul swoop

Now in its place
the shackle of shame

Witchcraft unleashed
The spell is cast
The belief
love lost to despair
Relationship endangered
The bond destroyed

All in one moment
Something said
did
acted

The delusion
this one swing of fate could destroy it all
The desperate wounds of the child
Haunted by fear

day in
day out

The lack of love
The absence of care
The unavailable parenting
was all her fault
A narrative begun
Many moons before
Etched deep in the brain

When connection is lost
The valid reasons

Proved in reality
unable to be found

Innocent till proven guilty
This hourglass turned on its head
Guilty before charged
Blameworthy as a baseline

In a coven of lies
Breaking sacrament
Shame the cursive

This
the undeleted scratch
on the record

ASYLUM

To take the step
with a grip of fear screaming no
Dragging the reins in the opposite direction
A terror of intimacy has ruled these lands

Love
affection
touch
All held prisoner
below the surface

Given just enough sunlight
nourishment to stay alive
but never enough to thrive
or plot an escape

Hope dissolved in betrayal
Fear encroached like a living mold
Silencing the need
the longing
the hunger

In this prison of isolation
Vulnerability becomes a distant echo
Translated into weakness
instead of an undisputed strength
Desire the furthest ripple

The protective stance
To not feel pain
To not be hurt
To become stronger than the vulnerability of love
No need to ever
shed a well of tears

Discernment sours into despair
Courage turned catastrophic thinking
Vulnerability becomes protection
Grief uninvited
Love disallowed
All the reasons to weep destroyed

Until the dawn of reckoning arises

Where the courage to love
the risk to connect
to begin an intimate conversation
the welcoming of grief
becomes greater

Greater than the threat of intimacy

Greater than the desire to be alone

PIERCED BY LIGHT

Fear strangling its hold
Piercing the eyes
Blinding the light

As the sweet softening of spirit
unfolds into life

Tumbled by God
Shined by source
Held in love

A sentient being
delivered into humanity

The birth tunnel raw
Awaking the senses

Sensitive to touch
Too vulnerable
Too heightened

In desperation the radiance dims
The energy fractures
Shattered to the bone
as humanness engulfs spirit

The fragility quakes
Imploded by fear

Wide eyed
Imprisoned by form

All is quiet
All is still
The truth buried deep beneath a bedrock of survival

The heartbeat faint
Veiled and hidden from view
Many paths chosen
Many callings ignored

until now

A moment with unadulterated truth revealed
The dormant spirit liberated by love
Awakened by a witness

The shell broken
The wings unfurled

The heart soars as the soul stirs
No hurry
No mind
No thinking
Just a simple liberation of spirit

The courage to feel
The more there is of love
the greater the sorrow

A risk worth taking

As tears fall
the heart breaks open
into the truth of being
once again

NO MORE APOLOGIES

For a life well lived
tipping into the second half
New moons cresting the horizon

What served you before
now destroying who you are becoming

No more regrets
No longer needing to apologize
for eccentricities
for the neutrality of power

No longer shying away from the essence of truth
the love
the divinity
the freedom

What has supported the past incarnation
will now shatter what is birthing
For this world of darkness now reaches for the light
Solitude to partnership
Burden to joy
Fear to gratitude

Being trapped in the mind
finally surrenders
to the embrace of love

The distance between the head and heart
only a few inches of terrain
yet riddled with miles of blockage
Minefields
Lifetimes of fear and doubt

How long is the road less traveled
for the return home
from the mind back to my heart
To live wholeheartedly
Whole bodied
Integrated as one

The edges full to overflowing
An embodiment of worth
Confidence
Truth

Led by Source
Supported by collaboration
An abundance of blessed grace

No longer to struggle alone
to push
or apologize
for being who you are
for authentic expression

for being a sacred being
in a sentient body of humanity

YOUR TRUE FACE

What are your innate values
That which you came in to be
Those which will rise above all else if allowed
Your sovereignty
The domain of your Queendom
The majesty of your Kingdom

What you complain about
reveals your values
when they are disrespected

What you would die for
Risk your pride for
Override fear of consequence for
Work for free

These answers
The principles of your lifeblood
Your moral ground of being
What is of most importance
The original blueprint of who you are
The document of you in writing

To know this of yourself
The core worth of your being
The intrinsic values of your birthright
Your creed
Your religion

To become an ambassador
of what you know to be true

To live in the authentic nature of this Christendom
The return to the Buddha nature
To abide in the realms of the Sages
To live in this kingdom of heaven here on earth

This is the commitment to your life's purpose
This is the way calling you home

Yet first these values need to be known
They are the origin of you
To know them by heart
Unlearned
A grace unfolding in design

Inquire
Contemplate
Pay attention to your life
Your upsets
Your priorities

How you spend your money
your time
your energy
is what you truly value

These principles will become your Bible
your doctrine
Let them lead

Override your thoughts
Give you the resilience
to never succumb to your fears

Let them be the authority
The sovereignty of your domain
The foundation of your capacity

Never again lost
on the ghost ship of someone else's naming of you

Ever awakening
Rejoicing in these ethics

A vehicle for your truest nature
The ground of your being
Your essence of pure consciousness

This the most delightful
dazzling
blinding
expression of you

"The price of inaction is far greater than the cost of making a mistake."
~ Meister Eckhart

UNLEASH YOUR SPIRIT

Rest in stillness
and listen to the whispers of intuition

CUTTING TEETH

Habit
Unconscious bartering
seared across the brain
Conditioning on steroids

Familiarity
an old armchair of reticence
Archaic
Comforting in its mold
Tethered in history
Frayed in beliefs

Familial
A sleep state
Unquestioning

What was taught
Branded
Owned
The scraps on the table
left by another's doctrine
Pierced by cultural shame

Habit breeding contempt
Incestuous pathways in the brain
Train tracks of despair
The insidious desire
to cleave to the familiar

No matter its torturous nature

The world of the child collides
with the trained wound of the adult
Who is parenting whom

The corridors of anxiety
strangulating
Worry beads in action

What if
anxiety is not the feeling
Instead an unconscious survival mechanism
to bury
hide
disarm
a bigger emotion

a terror filled emotion
Believing this fever pitch will be the death of you

What if anxiety is the doorway
The breach to the opening
The breakthrough
to shatter the fear
to crack the mold
to distill the mind

To stand in the threshold
To walk

fall
trip
into an unknown unfamiliar territory
Into the abyss of feeling
which lies beneath

The emotions aching for healing
Hungering for attention
Desperate for triage

For the love of God
Question
Inquire
Shake down
What is true for you
Do these patterns of behavior invoke care or harm

Are they aligned with your deepest value
What is most important
Your doctrine
Your authentic creed

Return to a home base of love
Where worry
anxiety
can be revealed as a habit

An old way
A survival mechanism
Hell-bent on safety against

disorganized connections
dominating insanity

Begin your day in health
Plough the first line straight
for the rest to surely follow

In alignment with self respect
Spiritual nature tended to
Care and wonder for the body
Ease and grace for the mind

Resting in surrender
In the embodied arms of an embrace
for all the emotions to reside

Revered in acceptance
In tenderness
In compassion

until all the pathways
are dissolved back to love

WALK INTO FEAR

To walk into the fear
barefoot
naked

Untethered by the story

To walk into the dragon's den
To know the heat of that fire
To sit still in the presence of all that is dread

Let your breath be taken away
Exhaling the life out of you

and breathe
Breathe deep
into this pain

The discomfort

Into the separation

Into the dementia
of severing a limb
that is yours

To lay unabashed
with all the exiled parts
surrounding you

Call them home
with loving acceptance

Let the tongues of the flame
lick the skin

Lean in
Come close
Beckon deep

Sit in the stillness of the tornado
In quiet knowing

These pacing tigers
deadly
ferocious
yet they are yours

In the utter courageous heart
that is you

Stumble into their life
knowing
in your heart of hearts
they will not destroy you
They are you

Their fuel is separation
Their healing is love
Acceptance

The connective heart of compassion

Knowing they have been left untamed
untethered
out in the wild

Exiled
from the essence of you
Caged outside the temple
the sacred heart of you

Exhume their bodies
Call them home
Call them by name
The parts of you that fill you with terror

The parts of you birthed from a wound
The parts of you ravaged by trauma

Call them home
Allow their reality
Embrace their presence

The wild embers of your past
To mature
To belong
To exist without resistance

Invite these wild demons
bloodstained

scarred
ravaged

To lay their weary heads
on your lap
and be loved

To become part
of the whole
of you

TEN THOUSAND ARROWS

The poison arrows of shame
of judgment
of criticism

The darts thrown
out of the other's
inadequacy
fear
protection

or the rabid terror
of being caught in folds of deceit

Desperation
to not look at their own deeds
Throwing mud
where ownership is unavailable

Daggers thrown
Fingers pointed
to deflect from the truth
Conspiring blame onto another

The first arrow may hurt
May even ring a resonance of truth
Yet the second arrow
as the Buddha declared

The one that causes
more pain
more suffering
Keeps the knife edge
burrowed deep within the psyche

The second arrow
The ten thousand arrows after
You have become the archer

The horror story declared in the mind
Believed
Wrapped in barbed wire
Engulfing the original pain
You are guilty
You were wrong
Spiked with self blame
The secret weapon

When pathology is no longer a warning
The true nature dissolved in narrative
The sickening thud to the stomach
The mind decays the truth

Drenched in story
Internal toxic worlds
believed as true

The first arrow hurts
The second arrow lies

This perception birthed from the wound

The serum straying
Lost in the pain of experience
Adding a harrowing portrait on top

In keeping the arrow lodged
the venom spreads
Scar tissue forms
The savage belief this is who you are

Yet when the second spike lands
filled with plague

In consciousness
With awareness
Held with compassion

A choice is made
to remove the crown of thorns
before the poison spreads

HIDDEN

What has been placed in a casket
buried deep below the surface

Left to rot on the clodded
cold earth of the unconscious
Undisturbed to die a death

Yet at times a faint stirring
A haunting of the dead
Old memories awaken
Trauma rising up for air

What if instead of turning away
A moment was taken
A step taken in the direction

A pause
to stop
to be still
to listen

What is unearthing
Who is calling for help
To be exhumed
Brought to awareness
Loved
loved some more

Cradled in such tender arms
Retracted back up to the light

Yes, trauma changes the brain
Yet so does healing

MERCURIAL

If avoidance no longer rules
The fall into the abyss of connection
may trip its way
into love

The heart cracking open
the guarded prison doors of survival

The experience finally safe
Not even about the other
Deeply
Richly
Potently
Unharmed within the true nature
in the commitment
to not abandon the self

Yet as detachment
releases the steel grip on the reins
Then
a fiery fuel of anxiety
pours gasoline onto another raging fire
In the past kept controlled by not engaging

On a cellular level
a connection felt
The back of the hand
the terror of being abandoned

A visceral memory
A need for love
A need for affinity
The infant's cry meets a ghostly quiet

The cavernous abandonment
Branding its mark
A smoke-filled room of emptiness
Shards of glass
scar paper-thin cuts
across the bandwidth of the psyche

Leaving it fragile
Exposed to the elements of others

The child unsafe
Searching for mother
father
surrogate
anyone

When the attachment forms
A crucifying hunger
devours the moments of connection

The harrowing need
Poisoned by emptiness
Wreaks havoc as soon as the bond is lost

The torturous infantile belief

Belied by accuracy
They left because of me
There is something wrong with me
It is my fault
If they do not choose me
I will die
I will do anything for them to stay
If they leave
I will die

The deeper the transference
The greater the terror
Value poured into their hands
Power at the mercy of another
Worth relinquished to their bidding
Respect ignored to gain favor
This born of fear
not love

Until the day arises
when the tormented child soldier
defeated in defending herself
is met by the parent residing within

The pain finally greater than the risk

Rejoices in unconditional love
with cradling arms
A heart of safety

The internal parental voice
A calming purr
A reassuring cradle song

I am here
I am always here
You are never alone
There was never anything wrong with you
You are loved
You are lovable
You are loving
I am here

This becomes the lullaby

A sense of safety residing within

Becoming secure within the self
where there is simply no risk at all

A RETURN TO INNOCENCE

Little one in hiding
For so long
All alone

Sweet child of mine
Burdened heavily
with a life not of your making

Grown-up fears
Adult responsibilities
left in dungeons of survival

Fix
manage
save
push
control
fear
A vigilance beyond your years

Never enough
No one to hold you
or soothe your terrorized heart

No space for surrender or faith
Only the night's watch

So little
yet needing to be big

Add weight
Be serious
Become the guise of the parent
Work harder
Be more
Hold it all

You are so very tired, little one
Spread thin
into the cut-out vigilance of an adult

A child acting grown up
Precocious, some might say
A pretense of control
Inauthentic in shackled bravery

A child soldier on the front line

Yet what choice was there
but to be a child in an adult body
A sheep in wolf's clothing

Such deep sorrow for this path forced upon you
Prayers
you now give up the burden
the weight
the responsibility

Give it back to its source
The parents
The ancestors

Back to the ones who are big
You are the child
Be the child

In this final act
turn back to wonder

Return to the innocence

you once lost

STAY CLOSE TO ME

Which words
would bring comfort
Solace to the fear
The night terrors
The rising anxiety

What, if said
with sincerity
heartfelt commitment
authenticity

would calm the infant
the child
the adolescent
caught on fire

What words, if offered
sanctioned
meant
Might begin the breath again
Calm the nervous system
Allow for safety

Give just enough courage
to enter the gnarly doors of fear

A lullaby
A reassurance

All that was never offered before

By the wise one already abiding within you
unavailable in childhood
who did not exist before

Stay close to me
I am right here
I am always here
I got you
Take my hand, sweetheart
I am here with you
We will face this together
There was never anything wrong with you
You were the child
They were the parent
You are safe now
Come closer

With these prayers chanted
On behalf of the ancestors
All relations
A chorus of love abounds

We love you, little one
Grown one
Wounded one
Deeply
Unconditionally

We are sorry, dear one
Courageous one
Beloved one
For your suffering
For leaving you alone
For it all

Please forgive us
Generous one
Committed one
For any part we played
For being unable to heal
our own trauma
For passing it on to you

Thank you
Healed one
Sacred one
For your courage
Your willingness
Your capacity to heal
what we were unable to

Stay close to these relations
Stay close to these revelations
Stay close to these reconciliations
Stay close to the reckoning

The release of the victim
The narrative of terror

Your medicine is your power
Only your medicine can change what is inside
Find your medicine
Own your medicine

On these wings of love
Stay closer
to the truth

until no separation remains

LITTLE ONE

I walk softly
A whispering stance to my being
Leaving no footprint of the past

I hold your beloved purity in my hands
The touch as soft as I can muster
in this clumsy human form

I see your eyes
I feel your pain
I sense your terror
I cradle your sweet innocence of a face

Whispering sweet everythings in your ear
so the truth of the experience can be witnessed
the self blame
the shame
the utter terrifying loneliness

I am here, I whisper
I am here
I am here
I am here
Repeating this as a heart song

You will never be alone again
You now have me, little one

You now have a grown-up version of yourself
who knows the truth
A witness to defend against the trial

I ask you
What if there was never anything wrong with you

I feel you squirm below the bedrock
Your being shaken by a long-awaited truth
Starting to pierce the manifold

To rattle and hum
a structure
a belief
a programming
that you were left alone
because of something wrong with you

There
was
never
anything
wrong
with
you

An infant born into the mercy of dysfunction
A babe in the woods raised by wolves
Programmed to do anything
For love

For acceptance
For some mirage of safety

I will protect you
I will set boundaries for you

I am here
I love you
a fierce
protective
parenting
functional
love

I love you unconditionally
from the winged tips of my spirit
I am sorry
I am sorry for your loneliness
I am sorry for the trauma
of believing there was something wrong with you
all these years

This was done to you
You were the child
They were the parent
Innocence laid bare

I am here
You are loved
There was never anything wrong with you

Said again and again
until the truth deletes the old scratches
Builds a new foundation

The double bind of the experience of trauma
bottlenecked with the belief that you were to blame
This no longer the double-edged sword
which will cut both ways

You are safe now
You belong in the cave of my heart
protected
loved
You are free from the narrative of poison

This
was
not
your
fault

There
was
never
anything
wrong
with
you

I feel your fear beginning to melt
To soften nestled in my hands
The relief of thawing a horrendous lie

of coming back to truth
to innocence
to longing
to a hunger aching in your bones

to be loved
to be held
to be seen
to be known

Now with a crack in the seam of the lie
For the truth to seep in
to bleed between the lines

You deserve it all
You, little one
are the most important thing

As I swaddle you
in proof of life
in proof of care

CHOSEN

A quiet still voice
Whispers in between
the silence of meditation

As confusion reigns
The mind trailing
into the delusion
of an external paradise

Lost in the wasteland
of potential threat
Suffocated codependency
Desire twisted into
survival manipulations
Neediness birthed
from an empty longing

Power handed to another
The child
Desperate to be claimed
To feel safe
To belong
Projecting unresolved pain
If not chosen
The tainted belief
of not being enough

In this deepest darkest fear
The voice arises
Firm
Calm
With dominion
Sanctioning
Distilling down to the core
The truth
Choose you
Return to you
Take the blinding
step back
into yourself

No longer about choosing another
or being chosen by another

A need to be protected
Protect yourself
A need to belong
Belong to the self
A need to be loved
Love yourself
A need to be chosen
Choose yourself

In knowing one's worth
Meeting inner demons with love
Wrapping arms of kindness

Surround the naked vulnerability
baying at the hackles of the hungry moon

This chooses you
Returns to you
Parents you
Protects you
Respects you

Fall in love with the self
the ultimate healing
The deepest love affair

The still quiet voice
No longer a whisper

Choose you

METAL DRAGONS UNFURL

Trauma strikes its hand
Whiplash across
the face
the chest
the heart

The wound bleeds
The heart weeps
tears of pain grieving for innocence lost

Before this moment
the tender flesh of the mind
the body
the emotions
unscarred

Yet now the experience scribed on the tablet of life

The imprint branded into the cells
Layer upon layer of steel
The wound finds home
A lair in which to lick its wounds

Cellular memory is born

In health each cell buoyant
A drop of light filled life

In trauma the cell stores memory
Bonded in heavy metal
Birthed into tiny wrecking balls

A twist of light forms dysfunction
The rays of the cell diminished

The perfect circle
The sphere of vitality
Depotentized by lead pellets
lying heavy within the wholeness

Weighted
The disease carried
throughout the ancestors
the bloodline
through experience
The thunderous footsteps of death's march

Until the prayer bell is rung
A match is struck in a resounding call for healing

The fuse lit
Magnificence on fire
Coursing through every cell of the body

In this miracle the steel ball unfurls
The wounds scarred and etched on the flesh
become a swirl of smoke
lifting from the threatened skin

The branding of flesh
the armor
of battles fought and lost

The serpent rises
The snake released from her plated prison
Bonded in lethargy
Exhausted by the continuous fight

Once again
feeling
absorbing
remembering

This fire of spirit
This spirit on fire
Life force at play

The scars
the imprints
the torturous branding
Shed from form
Released into the ether

The battle wounds
rise effortlessly
to the glass ceiling of each cell

Caressing the edges
with an ascent of unconditional love

Softening the words
dissolving
as the cellular trauma
lives no more

The fuel is now burnt to ash
Smoke released of karma

The snake circles the flame
dancing
between the ripples of light
in the shadow

Movement at last
Breath everlasting

The wound heals in this ignition of life force
Presence returns into itself

Each cell now a drop of light
The lifeblood no longer
suffocated
in the story
in the narratives of ghosts past
The serpent no longer at war with sovereignty

Instead they dance as one
Enlivening life force
to its fullest potential

TO DIE FOR

Risk your life
Your breath
Your identity

The soul cries out in valor
Lay back your head
Expose your neck
to welcome the cut of truth's knife
The noose of reality's rope

Rather than dying a little each day
For others
For stress
For timelines

No longer slice your own throat
by not speaking your truth
Fail to attack and condemn your own fragile heart

Surrender limiting
your power
your potential
by defying your dreams

No longer sacrifice your own being
your innate truth
in severed tongues
as though you have died already

What on earth is worth your life

No longer to stand down
Keep your head held high
Your spirit soaring

You, dear one
You are worth your life and so much more

No more apologies

Become the one who sings
who dances
who howls

She is still alive within you
Feel her in your veins

The tongue of a young woman
Drenched in silence
Bound by behaviors
Needing to be liked

Aching to express
Cut to the wick

Be struck by faith and love

It is time to light her up
Catch her on fire

To shine in all her glory
To glow her beacon of light

Remember yourself
Return to yourself

What in this world
would you die for

Die
oh yes
die a little

but only for you

DIGNITY

Meet your sufferings
as an old dear friend
standing forlorn and tattered at your door

Meet them with dignity
Fold them in tender arms

Welcome their fears
their grief
their pain

Pull them into your breast
Into your heart
Breathe them in close
Closer still
until no separation remains

Allow intimacy to melt all boundaries
Love and compassion to overwhelm
wrapped in weapons of surrender

Draw your sorrow even closer
Let it whisper in your ear
Soften the stance
Distill the resistance to push or pull away

Come closer to this beloved pain
Lean in

Be still
Courageous in despair

Become one with the ache
dissolving in the heart of acceptance
Become a mirror on the inside
Intimacy beyond words
Connect with the mourning
Unite with what is vital

The plateau where truth is all that resides
Allow connection to evoke compassion
as is its way

Melt
Drowning in the piercing matter of the heart
Commune with the truth
Call it by name
Noble in its cause

Imploding resistance
Dissolving judgment
Releasing the grip

Come closer, dear friend
Closer still
to your essential nature
behind the curtains of separation

FAITH RESTORED

Righteous indignation becomes righteous rage

A fighting stance held
in experience
in beliefs
Programs become the story

Stubbornness infiltrates the cells
morphing
twisting
until no cracks remain for the light to shine through

Shackled
Starved of love
of being seen or heard

The only choice left to fight and defend

Teeth bared
claws drawn
never turn your back

Human animal drenched in torture
cornered in filth
caged in familial shackles
An opening offered
a portal to healing
a release to freedom becomes the threat

The doorway offered
yet the tiger does not leave the imaginary cage

The only way through
To cradle
wrap
pour love's tender embrace as a soft carpet
to rest the weary

A woven blanket
to soften the concrete below
A gentle hand on the heart
as nourishment for the soul

More love offered
softening the steel
melting the iron

Hate simply
love that was hurt

Acknowledge the hate
Respect the hate
See its purpose of protection

To reject those
whose job was to love
To preserve against those
who used vulnerability as a weapon

To distance from those
whose own pain becomes the threat

More love poured
Cradled in generous boundless grace

An offering to rest in this love
An offering to rest in this light
An offering to allow its gentle gestures to restore
what is whole

This day of all days

This love
unconditional
unchanging
unimaginable to the part
full of pain and suffering

This love stays strong
Always lapping at the doorway of hurt
Melting away the edges of stubbornness
born of survival

The perfume of love
The feel of love
The essence of love

This day and all days
This love is offered

to the child of you
to the spirit of you
to the crevices where the soul enters
We will pray
We will love

Until

until

your faith is restored

DISINTEGRATION OF WOUNDED WILL

Gather them home
Go find the orphans of trauma
out in the wasteland
Meet them on bended knee
Acknowledge their pain

With searing clarity
Understand the exile
The need to stay on the periphery
to guard the inner realms

These child soldiers
Fierce in their terror
Their tiny frames desperate
to make the outside world safe

Evicted of mother
Drenched in violence and neglect
Left prey to the predator
Urchins lost to boarding school
Banished to caretaking
Feral in lack of protection

With an overflow of gratitude
for their sacrifice made unsacred

Take them by the hand
Educate with care

This was never theirs to hold

Return them home into the fold of the sacred heart
The arms and body of the adult
Under the mantle of maturity
The guidance of spirit

At last in utter exhaustion
To rest in peace
To rest in presence
To abide in awareness
To live in the realms of love

To finally remain in the heart center
What was believed to be known
now suspended
Surrendered into truth
The desperate need to control disintegrates

The ice finally melts
Through the childlike hands
The clenched fist softens
The fingers uncurl with arthritic pain
until the surrender
of an open palm
yields
face up towards the sun

A shudder of a sigh heaves the body

Till you know beyond reason
there is something greater
Bigger than the sullied frame of terrified mortality

The sense of presence
Available
Pulsing
Fathomless

The heartbeat of the universe
Giving of blood
Life force
Direction
All that is beyond reason

Pouring grace
Until finally
with faith
with integration
becoming whole
unsplintered

Remembering the fathomless intelligence
Above the fear
Beyond the ego

Receive without agenda all that is changing
The capacity to accept
To not resist

Finally knowing the one reality
The ultimate wisdom to get out of our own way
To let the universe lead
To receive all the gifts
To no longer resist the way forward
The path offered
The way of least resistance

Wounded will
Human instinct to protect against the threat
Perceived or real
what is not safe

Beckon the truth
Call it home
Reach out a hand

With an army of spirit at the door
The universe behind the back

Resurrect what is true
Lay to rest the delusions

THE SPLINTERED SOUL

Re acquaint
Re member
Re veal

These shards
Splinters
tattered and torn

Ripped from the very seam of you
The confines of you
The heart of you

Where did these shattered tendrils die

Ravaged by trauma
Lost in conditions
Societal rules

Drowned by fears
Conquered by dominion
Traumatized by hatred

The soul of you
The heart of you
Lost to the ethers
Exiled to worlds unknown

Caged by beliefs
Where did you all go
These aspects of you
The community of you

As poignant as the breath
As vital as the sun

Invite them home
All the lost souls
The lost selves
The hungry ghosts

Soften the conflict
Embrace the whole
Pray for harmony
Retrieve your self

The hidden parts of you
The condemned
Starved from lack of love
Damned by judgment and pain

For once in a far while
A mercy occurs
Those forgotten
pierce the confines of the wound

Like star-crossed lovers
Immature
Alone

are released

The prisoners from their shackles
A sanctuary awaits

A retrieval of the soul

Know they are all you
Rejoice in their homecoming

Bring peace to all who enter

The serenity of you
The heart of you

as you walk all of yourself home

REJOICE

Dance into the sensations of your body
A portal
A doorway
with much to reveal

Release all inhibitions
Open yourself to wherever this movement leads

Listen to your body
This feminine is your vessel
your temple
your home

Listen to the whispering messages
What is this miracle calling to you

Without thought
where does this sanctuary called home
long to move

is it subtle
is it strong
is it on the inside out

Surrender to every part of your being
which desires to dance

Receive the movement
A gift of abundance

Allow yourself to be replenished by nature's flow
Allow yourself to be nourished
nurtured
restored

Release the tension built within you
Soften
Surrender
Rest in the movement

Receive the transmission of your body
Become one with the beat of your heart
The sway of your hips
The flight of your limbs

Let the energy arise from the movement
Opening portals of light
Expansion from within

Allow yourself to express who you truly are
Know who you truly are
To become the essence of your nature
as earthen roots touch you
embrace you
become you

Allow yourself to receive the gifts
living throughout your body
The sweet undulation of the breath
to curl
meander through your being

The rapture of your feminine heart
 to flow and explore

As you dance to the sound of mother earth
As you beat to the drum of your own heart

Explore crevices
valleys of your being
Places never touched before

In this moment you are free
In this moment you are beauty adorned
In that moment you are who you came here to be

Be generous with yourself
Be transparent
Vulnerable in devout authenticity

Claim this experience
this lesson
this deep inner guidance
Born into form

Drop into your body
Fall back
Lean in
Become one with all of who you are

Release the mind
The inhibitions

Here lies the oracle of intuition
The ground of your being

Honor this temple
Love the essence
The aroma

Appreciate this sanctuary
for housing your life force
your spirit
your soul

Thank this mystery
for being the exquisite home in which you live
A space to express your bounty
your creativity
your love

You are your body
Your body is you

Dance your dance wherever you may be

Dance your dance

You are the Queen
You are the Lord
of the dance

said she

"Let come what comes,
let go what goes.
See what remains."
~ Ramana Maharshi

BECKONING

Into the mystic

A RIPENING

To pause the flow of this incessant life
To stop long enough to notice the world around
To be in relationship with what is
First the dam must be built

Chop the wood
Carry the water
Blood, sweat and tears

Spin the wheels

Cross the t's

Dot the i's

The faster the flow
The stronger the steel wall needs to be

Say yes to the pause
Lay claim to the stillness
Whisper loudly to the silence
Chant to Spirit
Talk deeply to the intimate heart

Build the pause

Dam the torrid rapids of the mind
Let silence become the loving vise grip

To contain and hold
To ignite such a deepening
stirring within the echoes of your soul
as to open the void
Face your demons and angels

An arising of reality
of who you truly are
Without
your life
your trappings
your trinkets

Without
your reputation
your tribe
your story

Build the steel trap so strong
to capture enough delusion
To be stilled
Brought to the light

Let the silence remain
pure
unadulterated
with infinite potential

Partner with the fabric of the universe
to burst through the walls of deception

Overflow the limitations
Flood the sleep state
with such a wash of awakening
that never again
will the giant of your being
be able to fall into such a stupor

Distill the truth
Pause your life

In order to fully live again

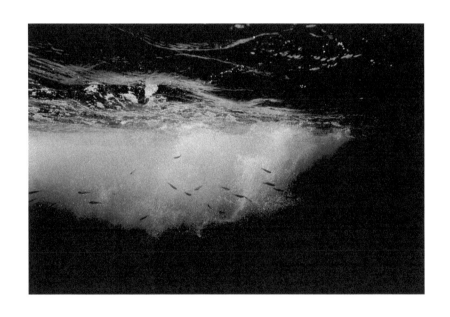

BROUGHT TO THE LIGHT

As you unveil your true self
more light will stream through

As you pull back the curtain of lies
Unfold the denials
Your own true radiance will pour forth

As you choose your authentic truth
over distortions lived
you become luminescent

Yet this light
in all its majestic glory
also lives within the shadows

As the vessel of your being
fills with illumination
vehemently shining upon the darkest corners

The broken spaces
The cracks in the foundation
The bleeding wounds

All that has been banished
hidden from view
will be brought to revelation

In this union the real work begins
The partnership of dusk and dawn
basking
in newfound liberation

To finally betray the hidden places
To lovingly cajole the fear from the shadow
To invite them all by name

Home to a newfound embrace of love
Drenched in compassion
No longer a rejection stance

Embrace the totality
All of who you are back into the fold
Only arrogance believes
these shadow sides should not exist
Ultimately this belief keeps loathing alive
In the resistance of exile
It gives the night terrors life

In humbleness all resides
All is welcome

In humility
the whole is embraced
In acceptance
it all just simply is

Welcome home the light and the dark
Revealing the buried treasure behind the veils

Honor the pain
cutting its teeth

Whispering into deafened ears
I am right here
Stay close
Stay close to me
Closer

Closer still

A LISTENING STANCE

I notice
the strangest phenomenon
while deeply listening

Not with my mind
or with my ears

Without expectation
Not even for an answer
when I just simply attend to what is

As though dropping below the brain
into the still lake below the surface
Beneath the commotion

The eyes fall inward
The attention alert
In a pregnant pause
Awake to listening

Is this not what we long for
To be deeply and intently perceived
To be heard without judgment
or agenda
or conditions

Give yourself this gift
Heed your own heart

Your own pulse of creator
Your own unfolding

Take any moment
This very moment now…

Still your body
Close your eyes
Shut your mouth
Become still
Become quiet

And begin…
Begin to simply listen
Listen to learn
Become the auditor
of your own experience

To what, you may ask
To everything that desires to express
To the silence
To whatever arises
To absolutely nothing
To it all

This
beloved
is where
grace will find you

GIFT GIVER

A tender intimacy
The intention
Render light to the shadow
A flame of hope
To see
Of being seen
To be known

Generosity in action
Risk yourself in giving
Knowing you will also receive

A call giver
Silently
lapping at the door

A heart song
A prayer of connection
Coverings turned back
Veils uplifted
for love to pour forth
A vulnerable
tender
act of devotion

Of giving
Not for you
but in a deep wisdom sense

Of giving
what will change their world
and in turn change yours

Release fear for faith
Isolation for togetherness
Loneliness for care

In this intimate vulnerability
The conversation begins
Continues
Deepens

Granting offerings
from the perfumed well
already overflowing

A bounty bestowed
The gift of providing
Intent to bring alive

A step taken into the heart
Anointing the life of another

THE DISCIPLINE OF TRUTH

Discipline
A harsh mistress

Emboldened with blood
Tattooed with dignity

The one with the whip of consciousness
who holds you to the bone
Pushing through the denial of lethargy
The shiny factor of lies
The glitter of addiction

In a moment of awakened madness
Let discipline become your friend
Repentance become your master
The Magi
The Sorcerer

The sword which cuts through the stupor
Let it hang low in the sky
A crescent moon of hope
The northern star guiding the way

Let the pain of discipline be stronger
than the pain of regret
Ask which causes more suffering

The torrid sting in the lie of yes
when spirit calls no
The resignation of blinding habits
Dictating apathy in lieu of action

The pain of longing
If only....

As on a deathbed of stone
Love ignored
Creativity bound

Opportunity lost
Kindness strewn

Wealth stored
People assumed
The body taken for granted

Prayers hollow as mortality beckons
The crescendo of habits
unconscious paradigms
The lost wishes of consciousness

A silent throb
The ache of being out of commitment with yourself
of not loving yourself
of abandoning yourself
of betraying what you know to be precious
What you know to be true

Forge authority like steel into the backbone of will

Dissolve wounded will into willingness
Invite discipline in as a disciple
Follow the lead of right action

Dissolve into desire
Embody your own agency
Become a sovereign being

Arise from the shackled shadows
The heartbreak of regret
Release the docile vengeful nature of shoulds

Practice restraint against harm
of yourself
of another
of this planet called home

No longer hover in the vats of shame
causing inertia
procrastination
and the stench of death

FREEDOM WITHIN FORM

To give structure
To provide a channel
A pathway
for freedom's chaos
is a paradox in form

Emancipation
left to her own devices
will flail
and spin

in a kaleidoscope
of directions

Unintentional in her devouring
Firelike in her hunger

Yet when given shape
A scaffolding of support
to intentionalise a sovereign path
The loyal hound stabilizes

For conscious choice
to run her fingers through
to ride on her wings
to flow through her banks

Discipline
Form
Rules

All words
which curl the toes
of liberation's rebellious nature

Still, the framework gives a course
nurtures the direction
curtails the floundering
True humility is knowing ignorance
Confessing the sins of control

While freedom left untethered
will ransom to the shadows
Enthralled in the chains of hubris

She will give the taste of the vine
Yet in a crushing crescendo of her fist
destroy the temple of worship

Abandoning the truth
to toil to no end

Give structure to her sovereignty
Allow this heart of desire
longing to find a home

Let silence be the design
The stilling whisper to set her free

Give of yourself fully
to the discipline
of intentional liberty

Then freedom will hold you dear
in loyal, loving arms
Released from bondage
Fueled by love

Channeled into the truth of integrity
Free from manipulations
No more restraints on your essential nature

WISDOM KEEPER

Unearthed
Brought to light
The universal intelligence of this world
seeped into the tender separation of it all

Earned
Given as a gift
at the end of the war

Blood
sweat
tears
All birth into the heart of the matter
This sepulcher of Truth

To bestow a birthright
Aging
Saging
Somewhere between birth and death
Discernment most high

Beliefs held
in the fists of righteousness
Sanctioned in the grip of fundamental morals

Stripped naked
into the heart of sincerity
The reality of experience

What if the clenched fist surrendered
fell into an open palm
of curiosity
of questioning
of capacity
of compassion

Be patient
Be still
Know the belief is a story

Words
Concepts
Simply the finger of God
pointing back to actuality

Listen
Be present
Pause the momentum
Be pregnant in the experience

Allow the encounter
To pierce your heart
Tenderize your muscle
Bleach your bones

Listen into the silence
A requiem of unadorned intensity
Intuition's birth song

Then and only then
is the wise
truly alive within you

BONE YARD

To walk the shadow with courage
Patience at the heels

In devotion's prayer
Committed to the wellness of the whole

The ancestral sovereignty
distilled in the family constellation

Melting the ice shards
until the waters purify the pain
the story
the unmet trauma

To succumb to the dominion
The support of the ancestors
Living strong behind your back

In gratitude for this life
In the relinquishing of carrying what is not yours
In the return of heavy destinies
The fates of those gone by

Returning it all with love
In kind receiving love back
Asking for blessings as the wheel turns differently
Taking the step against the self
programmed by the past

Call on this wisdom
Forgive the limitations

Be grateful beyond reason
 for all that has been sacrificed
All the love beholden
For the lineage continuing to unfold
For this gift of creation embodied as you

*"I need to be silent for a while,
worlds are forming in my heart."*
~ Meister Eckhart

THE RECKONING

Pregnant emptiness

THE FALL BACK

A systematic fear of pain
Leaves the psyche circling the drain

The terror
if allowed to spill into the abyss
the pain will not end

The free fall into sorrow
Trauma
The loss boundless
Infinite in its rapture

This is the fear
which never allows the step in

Yet in the witnessing of love
Being held in the tender arms of support
The fall back is taken
The foot lifts courageously into the void

The snow angel
spills her way
into these heavens of darkness

Then and only then
A curiosity occurs

The pain is momentary
A thrust
A deep blackened plummet
that lasts but seconds

On the other side
of this tremor
the void awaits

The silky absence of light
Beyond pain
Beyond reason
Beyond humanity

Who knew
pain
was the doorway
when swaddled in surrender

To enter pure
unadulterated
consciousness

AMISS

Attention given to achievement
The exalted climb of the ego
Solace in the physical body
Resilience in the mechanical mind
Determined control over the emotions

These steel girders
Devastate
Destroy
the tender scaffolding of faith

When a ghostly silence
echoes
in the chambers of the heart

The desperate search
collides with emptiness

Faith rendered lost
A haunting
in the shallow graves
A life half lived

Hope draped over humanity
The new gods fall short
as do the old

Religion suffocating love

Doctrine paralyzing truth
Scriptures distorted by man

Faith left immobilized
Desperation
the alchemical catalyst
Until the door unhinged
falls back to earth
Finally free

Devotion over proof
The silent whisper
Seeded deep within the heart
A confidence
Meaning
with faith

The conviction in what is unseen
Yet not blind

Merciful
filled with grace
Then faithfulness spreads her wings

Polarity no longer the creed
The abyss
pregnant with clemency
Restored
Bestowed
in a tapestry
of spiritual conviction

Patience the ally
Perseverance the courage
Until the throne of doubt
is overthrown

A newborn choice is made

Trust birthed
once again
in the unknown

SURRENDERED OF WOUND

Allowing the uncharted waters
of deep pain
heartache
sorrow
to bleed their way back to the shore

to be resolved
witnessed
completed

The scratch on the record
playing again and again
In the unresolved need for mercy

Feeling all that is not true
Nor real
No longer relevant to this moment now

To be finally washed with love
Bathed in compassion
Met with the safe ground of being

Call the wound in close
Closer still
until no separation remains

Healing is the tending of the wound
Suturing the memory with precision

Cleansing the story with care
Medicating the trauma with wisdom
Protecting the truth with discernment
Bandaging the salve with love

The patient belongs to the human self
The one who can be hurt
The one with blood in the water
The healer the centurion
The true essence which can never be harmed

Abide in this awareness
Freeing the old unfulfilled traumas
living on the periphery of life

Predictive with fear
Let them be met
Returned home
the connective tissue of compassion

No longer living by the default of the wound
Know this pain forged a merger with reality
Liberating from the delusions of stories past

A sense of well being
Finally at rest
in the allegiance of what is true
Orienting life
with consciousness affording choice

Release distortion
as you attend to the experience happening now

Rest in the simplicity of being
here
now

This immediate experience
This is the truth of awakening

Revealed
Revered
in the release of illusion

GODHEAD

Dissolve the content
The trailings of the mind
reaching far and wide
into thought
memory
desire

Living in deluded separation from this moment now

This view of opposites
causing a rupture
Inflamed instability
Limiting the capacity
to embrace reality

Change being the only constant

The narrative playing on the screen of the psyche
Resurrections of what is no longer
or will never be

A construct of thoughts
The conceptual mind
ideas
habits
addictions

A random passing thought
An itch in the brain beckons to be scratched

When felt with emotion
Enters the body
Falling fast into a distorted reality

The discomfort heralding the creed
Avoid the truth

Yet this

this...

this moment now

this
is
it

Awareness living behind the eyes
Consciousness mercurial in flight
The breath rises
The breath falls from presence

The heart beats
The eyes see
surfacing from awareness

Experience moves
Soul values honored
Birthed from consciousness

In the deepest of questions
Who am I
The simplest of answers
I am presence

The Godhead
Surrender to the oversoul
The divine source of being
The unknown aspects of spirit

See divinity in the ray of the sun
The horror of the news
The moonbeams at night
The sorrow
The goodness of humanity
See it all
as children of the divine

Bow to the Buddha
Deep gratitude for Christ
Reverence for Saint Teresa of Avila
The courage of Meister Eckhart
600 years before his time
For those mystics who went before us
who faced the suffering
who sat below the Bodhi tree

who died on the cross
who honored the Sacred above all else
who risked their lives
who gave their lives
who lived in truth

So we may sit in peace
Speak without fear
Teach without regret
Embody without persecution

In each moment come back to the here and now
Become aware of losing the present moment
No longer get lost in thought
Lying in wait for a future never to be seen

Free your soul
by burning back to the ground of being
the attachments
the memories
in pregnant emptiness

Let this be a welcomed hell
to set your soul free

THE UNREAL YOU

Suspend what you think to be true
Lay her down
naked
in the actual truth

Confess what you do not know
On bended knee
to the almighty
infinite consciousness
of being

Why invest
so heavily
in the unreal you

The fears
The doubts
The delusions

Opposing reality
In this argument
you will never win

Change the direction
Choose another way

Question
what is this unbounded love
which the body cannot contain

Who are you in the truth of your being
This being strong medicine
if you genuinely desire to know

Let the wonder
The devotion
The call

Ring beyond the limited realms
of the human form

Surrender to the truth
of all that you do not know

Who remains in the not knowing
with all archetypes set free

Lean back into
the tender remembrance
of innocence
Initiate again
A beginner's mind
Awake
Pure
Unveiled

Fresh to the pulse
of
this
moment
now

TUMBLE YOUR WAY BACK

Tumble your way back
to stillness

Fall deeply into grace
Into the still point
of simply being

Snow angel yourself
into the deep dark depths
of a tranquil lake
plummeting
falling
dissolving

Allow the eyes to fall back into the head
The jaw release the tension of being heard
The body the pressure of being seen

Feel yourself surrender
Give up the fight

A yawning
A dissension
into the heavy laden
energy of this earth
from whence you came

A molten liquid lava
pours through the veins

the bones
dissolving your mind

Disintegrating
all that is not
in existence

What if
for a precious moment
you ask
with an innocence
the curiosity of a child

Does this thought actually exist
if I stop thinking it

In that wrinkle in time
you are free
from the shackled
story knots
of the mind

Surrender yourself
to the stillness
to this quiet

To allow the world of consciousness
to hum
exist
be present
with or without you

In this instant
your only awareness
is to fall
into the apex of stillness

Beyond the heartbeat
Deeper than the breath
Wider than your thoughts

Descend into the still point
of presence
of being
of you
Into the void
The darkness

Be courageous

Know this is simply you
returning home
to the pulse of creation

Before you thought you knew

Know as you surrender
release
relinquish
your little steel fists

This world will continue to turn
Gravity will continue to hold

Infinity will continue to be boundless

Plummet back
into what you know to be true

You are a part
of this endless energy
This immeasurable potential

The conscious or unconscious
living or dead
Tears of laughter
Tears of pain

It is all the same

You are
You exist
You are worthy

simply
because you exist

Beyond reason
Beyond doubt

Love is the tapestry
A thread of heartbeats
The human connection to this pulse
This Om of all of creation

Take down the scaffolding
the structures
the laws

The regimes
that sear your mind

Relinquish the fortified grip you create
The fear
The ego's ambition
Desperate for accomplishment

Tear the tiles off the roof
The walls
The container
you outgrew
a thousand moons ago

and fall
let go

Yield deep and far
into the abyss of this moment now

There is nothing to do
nothing to fix

nothing to change
nothing to become

Simply more of your truth to be revealed

Allow a moment
of pure unadulterated beingness
To simply be
who you are

Now

Allow the creation of your body
Your character
Your astrology
Your ancestry
to course deep within your blood
your bones
your cells

Accept
Rejoice
Allow it all
Call it in close
Then cast out the nets
Surrendered to the vast ocean of emptiness

In its glory
Its magnificent brutality
Its vulnerable fierceness

Consent
with the permission
of love

To be whole

To be you
To be unconditional
Know what is true
What is in alignment
with your sacred nature
Releasing all that was taught
constrained
limited
out of fear
pain
or trauma

Remember
who you are
when fully embodied
in your own light
your own nature
your own values

your laughter
your sensuality
your power

Know you are
a child of God
a child of this universe
a child of the divine

always whole
already absolute
born unblemished as you

An expression of yourself
as creation itself

Of consciousness
simply dancing within your body

as a way
to awaken awareness

Move closer
as a child to a mother's breast

Suckle long
Drink deep
from this well

From what you know
to be true
in your heart

Drink the warm nectar
Inhale deep
what is already within you

Choose not to leave

this sacred space

forever

*"I felt in need of a great pilgrimage,
so I sat still for three days."*
~ Hafiz

PILGRIMAGE OF SILENCE

The quietness of being

ENTER YOURSELF

Your spirit awaits you
in a deep patient embrace

The essence of your true being
pauses gently
between worlds
breaths
passions

A pilgrim
Walking the path of in between
Stay loyal to not knowing
Taste it in your body
Revealing your true face

Your authentic nature
That which already abides
Just as death awaits you
so does yourself

Compassionate
in all the ways you leave home
Confident in your resilience
to always find your way back

As spirit folded into form
Stepped into your character

Your blood
Your marrow

The wings of your being
always behind your back

Remembering
A resonance
in the gentle contours
of your precious landscape

Draped
in a tender sigh
of this return home

ACTS OF CONSTANT RENEWAL

Pierce a moment
deeply
The epoch of new beginnings
A spear through the heart

So intently
that you dissolve
Becoming the experience with all your body
all your mind
all your being

Choose any moment
A hug
receiving a gift
watching loved ones

The drenching rain
A bird's wing
The opulent sky

A moment of quiet

and dive deep
swim long

Drink into the well of mystery
Quench your thirst

From the drought of past living
The starvation of future longing

Redeem this moment now
Open to the penetrating awe of consciousness

Let this be your gift
To be stilled by the poignancy
of this rendering
As each new moment begins

Again

and again

and again...

SPIRIT UNFOLDING

When the red thread
of human desire
becomes unbearable

Yearn
Say yes
Scream no

Pray
Meditate
Be still

Retreat
Study
Inquire

Seek wisdom
Knowledge
Answers

Purify
Transform
Initiate

Evolve
Expand
Become enlightened

Such light
Such consciousness

Too awake
Too bright
Retreat to the witness

Separate
Unattached
Observing from the ethers

Feels dull
Too dry
A longing to dance with spirit

Such joy
Undying bliss

Rich lavish adornments of God
The feast of devotion awakened

Grace
Echelon
Agape

To experience all as the infinite

You
me
the stranger

You
me
the torrid

You
me
the radiant

All still human
yet always infinite

Let the dance within begin

Falling back into the arms of boundless potential

Awakened to the divine emptiness

THE POWER OF SILENCE

A sunrise
without a timeline

A day
opening
blossoming
with pregnancy

Beauty adorned
Rolling
Filling
Emptying
as waves on the breath

No agenda
No pressure
No predictability

A heart and mind open
to the energy at play
to the sound of silence

Inviting stillness
Surrendering to inspiration
Deeply listening to intuition

Sitting
Loafing
Resting

Intent on the butterfly's wing
The bird's song
The breeze on the cheek

Empty, dear one
Empty
Empty some more

Until the floor falls
out of your mind

SPILLING GRACE

A fever pitch of presence
Mirrored
as the mind devotes service to the heart

A smile cracks forth
any residue of ego
or forgetting

As humbleness pours
across the threshold of life

Reverence awoken
to this present moment

Spellbound in a magical mystery tour

Transparent to the eye
Vapor thin to the touch
Lost and found in the wonder of this instant

Weaving silence into words
A wisdom hushed through the ages
Biblical in its reverberation

Lacing stillness into actions
The body becomes
the teacher
the messenger
the guide

The doorway through which
you are found
returned
remembered

A pause of presence
cries forth

The silence singing louder than fear
The heart's grace fuller than beliefs

Fill into the stretch
Surrender the mind to the heart

Let your mind become faithful
to the quiet hum of intuition
to the wisdom of your essence
to the discipline of your values

and spill
spill back

as you fall
into grace

*"I will always lean my soul
as close to your heart as I can."*
~ Hafiz

LETTERS OF LOVE

Vulnerable conversations with devotion

WALK WITH ME

Let me love myself
as you love me
The tapestry of this universe
Abounds
Abides
Birthed from love
No one stands alone

To remember
To embody
The ancient self
The blueprint of original design

We are all indigenous
Birthed from this earth
Born from creation
Bathed in love
Steeped in compassion's medicine

To call on the ancestors
To invite home the support of the well ones
To live in heartfelt gratitude for the gift of this life
To receive the blessing of a life lived differently

For the miracle of the lineage surviving
The many souls born from love

This precious conception which is you
The blood of the ancestors
still coursing your veins

BELOVED

As the divine masculine
unites with the divine feminine
Entwined in precious moments of connection

Chosen within the north star of integrity
Desire resounding to a wholehearted call

Sovereignty
the principal foundation

Freedom
the commitment

Invitation
the spaciousness

Compassion
the acceptance

Unconditional love
the foundation

When the laws of karma
No longer rule
No longer choose relationship
No longer living under the hand of destiny

A connection is birthed
A communion in spirit
A partnership prepared for

Chosen from Dharma
Divine law
In alliance
In accordance
with the decree of highest nature
Human animal uninvited
Conditionality refused

An integration of souls
In moments of togetherness
In times of separating
All as one

The love unbound
Space irrelevant

Sincere hearts fully present
Resting in illumined luminosity

These highest realms
devoted to love

A GLORIOUS INSTRUMENT

To adore you
Sourced with respect
Doused in unadulterated love

The cherishing of who you are
The nature of who you have always been
The unfolding of who you are becoming

A path of vulnerability
Beckoning its hand into the unknown

The guiding light
Intuition grounded
within the truth of the body
Overriding the strategic mind

If indifference is the enemy
To love deeply the medicine
To love unconditionally the alchemy

All that is unrecognized
All that is unknown
All I cannot know of you
All of which
will never belong to me
or ever belong to you

Born into your own true nature
An unfolding
A revelation of kind

To protect what is true
To protect the innocence of love
from harm

The choice made
in the deepest of highest domains
To see you
To listen intently
to the whisperings of your soul

The commitment
to rest in each other's devotion
This glorious instrument of you

To love
To treasure
in the deepest of mysteries
Meeting the stranger within

The offering
Let me never curtail your freedom
As you never diminish mine

Let me rest in the celebration
of unleashing your spirit
in a dance of liberating mine

Welcoming home
All the unknown parts of you

In doing so
Welcoming home
all the unknown parts of myself

THE AWAKENED HEART

Devout in authenticity
Without reason
Devoid of fear
or falsehood

Embodying a fierce love
A war cry
pouring forth

For compassion
For kindness
For service

This wise devotion
Bare breasted
Sacrifices the ego
The conditions
The story

Sets fire to the anger
The hatred

Burns down boundaries
Constrictions
Imprisonment

The purest of hearts
Unable to pierce
anything but love

Dissolving
all that is not true

The antidote to the poison
of hate
of fear
Trespassing
on the confines of restrictions

Revealing the glass ceilings
Conditions
Justifications which prove righteous pride
Drowned in human limitation

Crack open the merciful heart
Pierce it to the bone

Reveal the awakening
The fierce grace
The Pandora of love

Uncoil the serpent
Unshackle the chains
Untell the story

Be fierce in the face of fear
Pierce the heart of the matter

The heart of love
The beloved true heart of you

MERCY

Thank you for the opening of my heart
Thank you from the softening of my body
Thank you to the essence honoring all that is love

As I meditated last night
As I meditate again this morning
Sleep elusive
Faith arose

Hope as a vehicle for love
Weaving back together
in a tapestry
of this world
this universe
as love

Piercing the veils
The exiled parts made whole
An invitation back to what is true

For the scar tissue
where love has lain bleeding
This nectar enters
pure
unadulterated
potency in form

A seamstress of the Divine
Divine Mother
High feminine
Healing
all that is not love

As the brain seared by trauma
is relieved of distorted pathways
The story dissolving
in the cohesion of sanctity

From the wisdom of the sages
The seers
In the deepest of gratitude
for the purity of love to be revealed

The mantra echoes its medicine
Laying new pathways in place

I am
I am love
An embodiment of love

Whispering into the silence
An echo of acceptance
A resonance of truth

God is love
Love is God

THE BONES OF THE FATHER

To father
To being fathered
To fathering

To the father we know
To the father never known
To the grandfathers
To the great-grandfathers
To the bones of our fathers
The great spirit of our ancestral fathers

To the archetype of father
To all who have fathered before us
To all who will father after us
To all who stand behind us
To the father within us all
The forefathers

To the provider
To the protector

To the fierce love
To the tough love
To the absent love

To the gift of learning that came from father
To the gift of independence taught by father
To the embodiment of boundaries led by father
To the deep well of feelings hidden by father

For those blessed enough to be cherished by father
For those courageous enough to stand up to father
For those graced enough to be adored by father
For those resilient enough
to survive the grief of father
For those strong enough to survive no father

For those resilient enough to finally
forgive
father

For the high masculine
For the low masculine
The patriarch

To our father
For all that is
For all that ever will be

For the potent seed of life
Sired
that became us
given by father

For this season of life
A precious gift
to be held in appreciation

of father

A MOTHER'S LOVE

Is there such a language
to express the power and beauty of a mother's love
The strength
The devotion
The care

Are there words to express
such heroism and majesty
The bearer of joy
yet also such sweet sorrow
No longer immune to the pain of love

For as the child is born
so is the mother
Forever walking around with her heart
outside of her body

This passageway revealing courage unknown
Fears untamed
Nothing else invokes such a rich abyss
of happiness and sadness
reverence and exhaustion

For how on earth could a mother
invest so heavily in her child's world
without sacrificing her own

The pathway home
The forgiving heart

The patient sigh
Holding the hand for a little while
The heart forever

Divine Mother
we pray for balance
for wisdom
for discernment

We pray to the invisible mother
who is known so intimately within her belly
Yet cannot be seen

To the mother in us all
The earth
The surrogate
The great
The humbled

To the ancestors before us
The generations to come
Let us forgive the crimes
The sins
The hurts
The pain

Allowing the miracle of a mother's love
to be truly revealed
felt wholeheartedly

Grant permission for this love
to heal the scars
the stories
the righteousness
the trauma
of our own beginnings

We all have a mother
For better
For worse
Yet no other offering will ever equal
her most precious gift

The blessed creation of life

Let us revere the miracle of a mother's love
To ring true throughout our lives
Resounding in our hearts
To birth the final steps of healing
To free the new life becoming

Forgiveness
The last step on this sacred journey

To all mothers
This declaration an offering to you
With a full heart
With joy
With love

All beyond words

Dear one
Already mother born bright
surrendered
courageous
overflowing with love

To bestow and behold such an innate yearning
To mother this little unnamed world

Resting in the cave of the heart
The womb held close
In arms which will cradle this soul

To promise always
To rise
and rise again

this little being
to the highest rock possible

RETURN TO HER

When love is unshackled
From the beliefs
The constraints
The conditions
The imprisonment of humanity's fear

When love is set free
To course through the veins
To heal all wounds
To emanate
Pouring life force into every cell
Every particle of this tapestry of life

When love is released
from the exiled room of delusion
Devotion soars
An eagle's wing on the currents of life

Love embodies the true self
Without agenda
Without fear
Without a grip to squeeze the living daylights
from this perfumed delicacy

Love held at its highest form in an open palm
An unclenched fist
The wretched fear released
The terror of abandonment no longer a threat

What is this personal liability being provoked
As the old way cracked in two
As love demands its new untethered
yet ancient reality

An agent of love
For each other

This

This is love

This the tapestry of the universe
from which all is birthed

Radiance at its most exalted

Why would we not lift
our hearts
our eyes
our whole being
to the crowning
and anointing

of this beloved

LOVE'S PRAYER

Heart of the Universe
Heart of Love
Who art above as below
Infinite throughout time and space
Sacred is your presence
which reigns down on this earth
Thy will be done
On earth as it is throughout the universe

As we surrender to reality
As we surrender to love
Our minds obedient and in service to our hearts
Give us this day our daily nourishment
An infinite supply of vitality and compassion
Let us live in a well of gratitude
for these gifts freely given

Forgive us our fears and prejudices
As we have mercy
for all those who wish harm against us
Lead us not into the temptation
of conscious or unconscious harm
Internal or external harm
Lead us away from denial
and towards our truest nature

Replace cruelty with kindness
Fear with love and understanding
Hatred with forgiveness

Deliver us from fear and judgment
for time immemorial
Let us live within the realms of deepest gratitude
Within the vulnerability of an open heart
An allegiance to a beginner's mind

Abiding in unconditional love
With truths revealed

Go with God

So be it

"The more in harmony you come
with the flow of your own existence,
the more magical it becomes.
Things line up in ways
you could never imagine."
~ Adyashanti

BEAUTIFUL CREATURES

Devoted pilgrims walking this earth

SEAMSTRESS OF THE DIVINE

Beauty incarnate
Threadbound

A seamstress of the divine
Weaving her scorpionic way
through this land

Full of humanity
Full of paradox
Her wings clipped under a blood red sky

Love is her fuel
Her potion
as freedom calls from the heights of her spirit

Yet a crash landing
of duty
of rules

even if a gilded cage
collide with the fluid form
draped in silk and threads
as she moves

her wings wayward
forward...

Her joy calling
Her spirit calling
Her kindness calling
Her love

Then and only then
does the river of divinity
move through her

A torrent of devout kindness
Full of heart

A wellspring
of care
of concern
of service

This beautiful creature
She would curl her limbs around you for warmth
She would lie beside you
counting stars and constellations
until you fall asleep

Her hands of warmth
Such healing powers
Her heart full of treasures
Given in pure delight
The presence of support
Unbridled by conformity

This she embodies
Overflowing
Unconditional
Untamed

A fierce
keening
love

MAVERICK MOTHER

Maverick mothers
Born and bled
with heart ripped open in love

Entwined in the mystery
The creation of life
birthed from love and connection

Running deeper than any thought
Any condition
Beyond reason

As two hearts collide
with the force of an atom splitting
A mother to a child
A woman to a life birthed
A matriarch to an innocent

Two separate identities here on earth
Created with the same genes
The legacy of the father growing inside
Bound in love
Desperate to remember
in spirit we are already as one

Maverick mother
Rebellious in nature
Pioneering the edges of parenting

Stripping down the conditions
The fears
The defenses
The judgments of parenting past

In a revolution
Back to the bare bones
Destroying the bloodlines of limitation

Teeter-tottering on the edges of vulnerability
Discarding what others may think

A free thinker
Autonomous
Independent from the norm

Seeing the child with a love of freedom
The light of who they are

Not through the lens
of contouring desires onto another

Surrendering
Releasing
Destroying the lies
The shadows past

Until the truth of this child's intrinsic nature
Stands strong in the light

Then the only possibility
to fall deeper in love
with such abandon
such absolution
as to release this force of nature
into life itself

To liberate
the agenda
the job
the responsibility
the ferocious will
of gripping fears and beliefs

Then it is known
This life before you is anything but yours

How this love
This being of innocence
is not a mirror of you
or for you to hold
or to own

Nor a potential to heal all wounds
The inherited distortions

To rise above ownership
The dictates of human possession

To set this deepest most cherished love free
To be their authentic self

To foster their autonomy
Their independent spirit

And in doing so
Liberate the conditions
of the mother's historical heart

To live in awe
with no regret

in setting the beloved daughter free

LOVE GONE EXPLORING

As though my heart has left my chest
Walking footsteps within yours
Pulled
Stretched to the far ends
of a Land Cruising adventure

To see a young child bloom into a woman
Independence soar to the four winds
Such courage
Such wisdom
Such will

An eye for beauty
Captured in the still of a frame
Nature engulfing the soul
The seeds from which we came

Back to earth
Into the wilds
As solitude becomes your friend

Wise beyond your years
courageous
fearless
unbound

What stirs you, beloved one
What captivates your heart

As you turn the bend into adulthood
Alone
Pioneering

As you walk the course
of your internal quest and compass

Who are you becoming
What phoenix will arise
I await with bated breath
An awe pulsing in my heart

A photographer
An explorer
A writer
The ocean your home

As you touch the hearts of many
Inspiring drudgery into dreams
An activist of care

Your devotion to life
To the infinite beauty of the earth's palette

Colors and creatures underfoot
Mountains eclipsing the view
Waters streaming
Stars silently resplendent
Such presence

Meeting people
In the essence of their life
tenderly colliding with yours

Points at the crossroads
A nod
A smile

With such deep gratitude for your freedom
Such grace to know and listen to your calling
To let mother nature mold and carve you
The beauty that is you

To reign queen of your dominion
To explore towns
cities
continents
Then breathe back into the vast expanse of the wild

To be held
Loved by dear friends
family
and released back to the void
Time and time again

You, my dearest one
Who boldly says yes to life
Who manifests dreams into reality
Who is loved more I wonder
than you will ever know

You, my daughter
My heart is always with you
A golden thread always connected
My faith
My trust
My prayers
with such respect and admiration

As you lay your heart
your faith in the land we call home
In her beauty
her creatures
her ruthless creation and destruction

Know my heart has left my chest willingly
Pulled by the love of your vision quest and journey
Overjoyed to follow wholeheartedly

that which is you

SARTORI

Always arising
even when you have it all
Wealth
Children
Family
Reputation
Power
Health

A nudge
a push
a pull
A thrust of knowing
There is more to this life
deep in the midst of your being

A stirring echo of discontent
As the tapestry of choice
weaves its beautiful facade
Covering the world beneath

You know it
You feel it
in the ripples of a stolen moment

A call and response
Quivering to the bone
Stirring in your soul
An intuition

to surrender the trappings
the conformity
the lies

To throw the rigidity of caution to the wind
Lessen the shackles of responsibility
To unleash what has behaved so well
To claim the autonomy of your own desires
Though not yet...

As though holding your breath
for the eternity of humanity
A deep wisdom
in knowing all will unravel

How five days of silence will unearth your world
Untether your sovereignty
Crack open your heart

To become the namesake
An embodiment of intuitive illumination

There will be no going back
My friend
My beloved

All in good time
All in Divine time

You will open Pandora's box
to meet who you truly are

SHAKTI

To a beloved child of the universe
A daughter of the Divine Mother
Steeped in Tradition
Birthed in the ways of the Sages
Born human
yet living beyond those realms

Curious
Devoted
Wondrous

Disciplined
Dedicated to service
To the lives and welfare of others

That light in your heart
shining stronger than judgment

A spirit
Fierce in Faith
Piercing the Truth
The Absolute
A beacon in this world of shadows
As polarized opposites return to one

Boundless
Infinite
Immortal

To us who love you
Blessed are we

To us who are loved by you
We abide in your Grace

Let the Shakti of Spirit
shine through
this human form

Allow the love and devotion
of your heart
to touch ours always

Surrender to the heart of you
The soul of you

Shakti personified
Beauty embodied
Wisdom adorned

May Divine knowledge
Illuminate you
Heal you
in a wedding dress of creation

May supreme knowledge
Baptize you

May radiant grace
Bestow on you

An inauguration of the Holy fire
Transcendent
Traversing all realms
All possibility
All limitations

You
dear one
are loved beyond reason

FIRE IN THE SOUL

Out of respect you dimmed your light
Out of decency you quelled the fire of spirit

A pause in the momentum
as history collides with consciousness

The pendulum swings
pausing at the pinnacle of conditioned behavior

In the still point
awareness cleaves a new way
An awakened stance finds ever existing footing

Yet this time was precious
to explore
to inquire
to seek who you are
Human nature colliding with the heart of decency

In the years of being judged
labeled
not seen

In lifetimes of being it all

In a need to understand
To drop back into human animal instinct

Programmed to judge
to discriminate
to hate

The experience vital
to acknowledge the drops of hate
lingering in each soul

To mitigate the fear
the terror
the rage
forever seeping under the skin

Hostility fueling the flames
Addictive in its seduction

To touch the face to the fire
of this reality
The cruel merciless nature
of humanity
This too had to be felt

What this earth needs is more light
The planet
humanity
needs more than ever
a man such as you
a love such as yours

Mistakes will be made
Awareness brought to more light
Yet ignorance no longer the master

Shakti burning bright
blinding the conditions
the stories
the narrative

until it is all burnt
Scorched to an ember
as the phoenix rises from the ashes

JOY

In her presence
we are assured

In her light
we are bathed

In her love
we are confident

In her faith
we are praised

To know this essence
we are blessed

To have this presence
we are rejoiced

Birthed from a bountiful heart
Spilling with generosity

Healed by grace
greater than any experience

A knowing
Deep within the bones

A presence beyond human
Spirit in form

Arising from nowhere
Inexplicable
Vulnerable in authentic expression

When bubbling up from experience
Nowhere to hide

This being of joy
Delight in form

If longing for joy
Look no further
Honor the presence

Joy
the emotion of great enchantment
is here before us
Within us
Surrounding us

Who loves us
Prays for us
Who cherishes
Who mothers
Causes healing

Joy is the one
sending you love
even when you do not know you need it

Intuition personified
Wise woman

A peal of laughter
Spontaneous in mirth

Let it be known
this gift we receive
is to be cherished beyond words

Embraced with might
Blessed to behold

Just as the Divine Mother
holds the world in her arms
yet loves with freedom
A fierce independence of autonomy

All that is pure of heart
This the embodiment of joy

BLOOD ROOT

Elder
Know you earned your place

The dog ears of experience

The cry lines
birthing a smile

The ache of bleached bones
inscribed with story

The blood
thinned by heartbreak

The skeleton
weathered by winds of time

Wrinkles in the brain
Scorched ten thousand times
over

A slowing of the heart
The longing
The desires as ambition lies breech

To the one who has prepared for death
by dying a thousand ways in life

As death draws near
This title is revered and honored by few

A receptor of the teachings
Of time gone by
As keepers of spiritual authority

Respect for the wise one
The oracles of time

Give care for the elder
as their precious life slows in motion

Love for the ones who birthed us pups
Who held the ancestral line
Who gave us life

Imprison the arrogance
Set gratitude free

Bow in reverence

to the strength
the lineage
the spirit wisdom

of our
tribal
ancestral
Elders

"The important thing is not to think much
but to love much;
and so do that
which best stirs you to love."
~ Teresa of Avila

HOLY

Acts of devotion
bestowed on hallowed ground

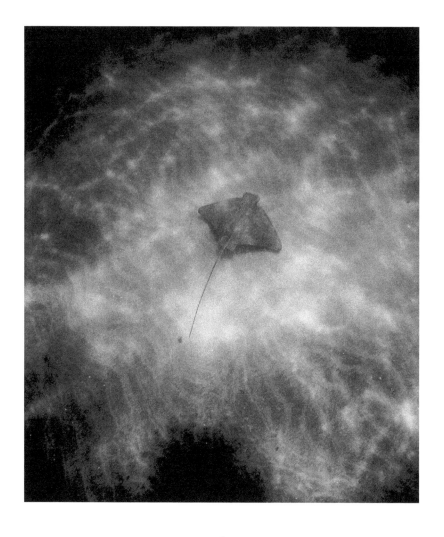

THE THAW

How could I not know
the grandeur
and beauty
of a lake's thaw

A coveted secret
beneath a canopy
of shedding leaves

The silent orchestra
uncelebrated
anonymous in her beauty

The frozen earth
cracks and moans
unnoticed

This majestic death
of her covered existence
is for no one

The ice
she groans in the breaking of her back

The spine flails
the undulating current of water below
bursting at the seams

Coursing through the exposed veins
on the lake's surface

The sun's laser
high in the northern sky
pierces the weakest link

Fracturing the splinters apart
breaking the molecular chain
in this fusion of fire and ice

The music begins
the splintering whip of the ice breaking her seam
thundering deep below
the cavernous underbelly of still waters

The fracture
shuddering
the bowels below

A whale's song
as distant as thunder
echoing up from the earth's core

A body of water
miles wide
This crystal maze
belching and moaning
the cracking of her surface

A belly full of eruption
as the seams split open

The frozen stillness
no longer captured in time

A sharp crack
as the sun whips her fire
again and again

Lashing the ice's surface
scorching to the bone
burning the flesh

until... until...
all breaks loose
unbound
thawed back into life

As I sit
eyelids closed
the orchestra has begun

The thunderous beauty
drums
bemoaning destruction

The sharpened high notes
of wind and wings
play on the life force of nature's threads

Then thunderous silence
pregnantly pausing the next eruption

Breaking the confines
which have been frozen in time
only heard
only witnessed

as my ears are there
listening
soothed by the stillness
attuned to the wait

Yearning for more
of nature's musical miracle

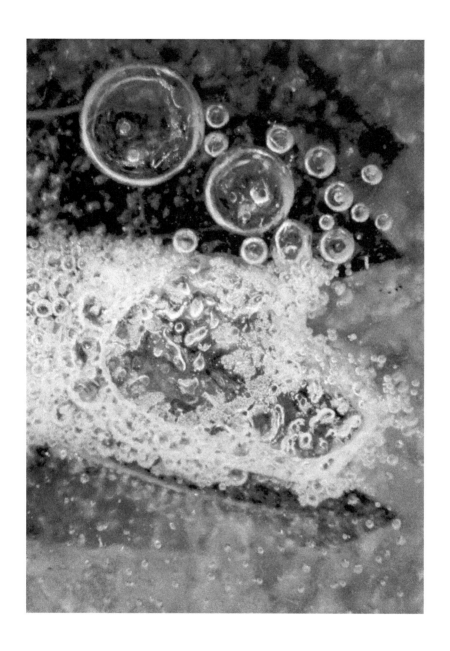

Photo by Birla Angelica

DESPERATE HOPE

The gift
The privilege
to be invited

into a glimpse
of the lives of Vietnam

Fragile hearts
Filled with fear
Scarcity
Lack

Isolated in a world of poverty
Alone in their hunger
For food
For hope
For change

At the mercy
of a harsh life
Families split apart

Dirt poor
betrays the dirt they lie on

The mother's one wish
for her child to have an education

Blood in her eye
Nervous
Hands wringing
So unsure

Is there help?
Will it come?
Are there grounds for hope?

Human animal
Caught in the confines
of human survival

Within a minute's walk
Along a mud-strewn
broken path

Heat
butterflies
jackfruit
coconuts abound

A cobbled path
to another world

One where help was offered
Fear was uncaged

By generous hearts far away
A gift of hope
by those who care

A gift of education
of training
of tools

So fully embraced
in earnest appreciation

An offering which changes lives
Changes families
Changes communities

As the tender hearts
of the Vietnamese people
are revealed

Once survival is pierced
to the bone
Risen above
Affording generosity to another

The firstborn chick or calf or piglet
Given freely to another family in the village
As the gift keeps on giving

A new way offered
Where love and caring
for each other
pours forth
from their own being

As twelve values
Cornerstones
Truths
are embraced
embodied

Lived by
Taught
Entrusted

The women the fire starters
in this transformation
Fierce in their ways
Fearless in their strength

Such smiles reveal broken teeth
Hands worn by work

Yet all fueled by
a newborn hope
a sustainable confidence

A cow
Some ducks
A sow

are the final gift
in a journey
Building a new foundation

Precious in its principles
Tried and tested
in the field

Two countries apart
Collide

in the heartfelt wish
to change this world

Inspired by a trip to Vietnam with Heifer International

THE HEART OF REIKI

Reiki
A gift of Spirit

Bestowed to those
whose hearts rebel against hate
against separation

An endowment from the fiber
of the universe
A benevolence
stirring what is already within

A union
A marriage
of the soul's purpose
Overriding the fears of humanity
Abiding in truth

To those whose hearts have cracked
into a thousand pieces
To you to whom much has been given
much is required

A requiem of love
The remembrance of truth
An offering for the mystic within you

Granted to the wild of heart
The spiritual revolutionaries

Revel in this grace
Live in gratitude
For the sages before us
The lineage of faith behind us

Fall into the heart of Reiki
Fall into the heart of love

Provide solace and counsel
Service exalted most high

Risk it all
Call it by name

To destroy all that is not love
To abide in the glory of grace

Remember beyond reason
the creed of truth
A communion between
the conscious and unconscious

A journey of awakening
Guided by divine intervention
Cradled in divine timing

For all truths to be revealed

The truth of being
Facing the mirror within

A direct meeting with the self
To thine own self be true

The rarest of gifts
to reflect this for others

To adorn
love
care
into tender hearts
with the Spirit of energy

SACRED HOOP

A sacred hoop
Caught on the wings of creation
Soaring high above the mundane
to call on Great Spirit

Birthed to heal
Devoted to the forces of nature
Sunwise in her direction

The medicine wheel
Crafted from nature herself
Elements
Prayer
Intention
The universe conspiring on your behalf

Unearth your struggles
Attune your vision
Realize your potential

A wheel of life
No beginning
No end
Aligned with mother earth
Destined to the four directions
A great vision in reverence to the mystery

Evoking the spirit of the seasons

Birthed in the East
A renewal of spring
Vision
Blood red victory
Soar on with the wings of spirit
The sun behind your back
Breathe into the instrument of you
Carry these prayers back to the Creator

The South, white beads of summer
Fertile abundance abounds
In union with compassion
The calling of the heart
Fire in the belly
As above and so below

Autumn's West
A black death of summer's cycle
The shedding of the snakeskin's bark
A deep healing
within the hidden earth caves
below the mountains high
To know who you truly are as the harvest is reaped

The cold North
Surviving the silence of winter
A howling echoes the ice winds
With patience
Dormant
Healing the past

Stilling your mind in hibernation
A call to go inward
All at rest
No more regrets before the thaw

Fingers
weaving
prayer knots

Time after time
Turning the thread

A web of protection
Unveiling the way forward

Weave your heart
Catch your dreams
Implore your desires
Burrowed within the depths of mercy

Your soul
Your dreams
Birthed inside this creation

Reveal your truth in the design
The flow of nature's beauty
Authentic in taking no prisoners

Tend to your devotion
Marry your soul's values in this fire of creation

Bestow yourself
Redeem yourself
Forgive yourself

Let this sacred circle
A hoop of life
Reveal your inner depths
Your silent calls
Your soul values
Your radiant beauty

To honor community
To abide in the mercy of this land
To live in harmony
With Spirit
With yourself
With others
With this earth

To be a wise steward of this world
This home
To give back more than you take

To come inside out
To lay open
an unyielding love
in the heart
of your own reckoning

BLADES OF FLIGHT

She hovers
A ten-ton weight of steel
Grounding her to the earth

Waiting
Pulsing
Pausing
with the weight of horsepower behind her back

Raising momentum
Her blades gather force
Filled with expectant tension

Steam mounts
The throttle on
The engines roar
Pregnant in tension

Building a driving force
until there is enough might for liftoff

A few feet above the earth's surface
Suspended
Twisting
Turning for the whole to fly

Every sense alive
A deafening roar to the ears

The earth vibrating
moving underfoot
The eyes wide
as the mounting beast looms larger than life
The nose filled
as dust ravages in an onslaught of occupancy

Higher
Higher

Lifting dirt
The earth rises to meet her
A direct north line
Straight up
Vertical to the heavens

She heaves
Lurching
A final strain upward

The pilot
Eyes on the goal
The way forward
The throttle moves
Higher in dimensions

The path ahead
A narrowing canyon steeled with rock

A rescue mission
Unheralded by fear

Sacrifice at its most sacred

Her wingspan
Poised dimensions only just able to fit

An inch to the left
the blade destroyed
An inch to the right
the same
Destruction

Such precision
The mastery at the controls
Hovering in space and time
Keeping the holy distance
directly in the center of the arc
A grace fills the air
A delicate balance
of human and machine in partnership

A misjudgment
death
A miscalculation
devastation

Suspended
in time
in space
A forward thrust
steadying the air

Precision in flight
In the heart of knowing
the steward's version of God

Concentration beyond fault
The higher mind in meditation
Fully present
Fully awake
Into the eyes of death

A distraction into the past
A glimpse into the future
The war is lost

The lesson, discipline
The law of staying present
Being centered

Aligned in the shaft of right action
Wisdom presents itself
Expertise refined

The air filled with momentum

A wildcat of metal
delays in wait
to pause
to pounce
to move at the exact right time

The giant feline
a breed of patience
a breed of presence

On pain of death
The canyon looms large
A bloated mouth
ready to devour whatever touches her sides

Subtle
Delicate

The giant beast with finesse glides forward
Confident with faith at the helm

The mouse whiskers touch ever so softly
knowing the edges of safety

A warning
for the preciousness
the fragility of this vulnerable life

A teaching for mindfulness
Harboring awareness

A captain of intentional design

OUR BELOVED CHILDREN

Our children
The future
The beloved generations to come

Not wanting to ground
Walking on tiptoes
Playing games of destruction
Drowning in technical devices

Why tether what is harmed
To that which is wounded
That which is dying

Eye contact avoided
Physical connection clumsy
Full sentences challenging

Numbing substances
Instant gratification

Parents as friends
Adults lost in addiction
Protectors gone rogue
Bellies hungry
Neighborhoods unsafe

These children drenched in anxiety
These innocents alive during wartime

Bloodshed against the homeland of the earth
A world not safe
The future uncertain

Yet not of their own making

This empty shell our children will inherit
Unhinged in madness
The parasites on fire
Ravenous in greed
Blinded in fatal mistakes

This is the spell cast
The delusion suffered
The legacy given

This the war crime
against our children

WHERE SHE GOES, WE GO

PachaMama
Who are these earth keepers
who place their hands on this world
in service
in gratitude
in healing
for these precious gifts of life
she so affords us

Where are these earth keepers
Who know
Where she goes we go
What happens to her happens to us
Her destruction is ours

This treatment of home
The disrespect of resources
A raping of what was never ours

These earth keepers are needed
Now more than ever
Reconciliation demanded
Reciprocity crucial
Prayers
devotion
action
no longer a choice

To place the hands palm down
on the pulse of this earth
On her heartbeat
On the sacred ground on which we stand

To feel the energy coursing through the body
from whence we came
To know we are one
Remembering we were born from this earth

Call on the feminine
Before time immemorial
Before she was
dominated
controlled by the patriarch

Call back the eternal
The ancestors who remember
who honored
who respected
who loved all of this earth

Earth is our mother
Our father

Without her
extinction imminent
Our children
next in line

The irony
Mother earth has no agenda
Whether we survive
If she survives
Simply another moment of destruction
in the fathomless
limitless
existence of this universe

Yet humans
Given a gift and a curse
Free will
Every moment a choice is made
To cause
love
care
honor
or
harm

When free will
drowning in ignorance
selfish in greed
reaps death's sickle

Beckons forth the Grim Reaper
with utter ignorance of the consequence

A childlike immaturity
The treats will simply keep coming

An ego frozen in a feeding frenzy
Individual action not deemed important

The teenager greedy
for saturation
satiation
Never looking beyond the consequences
of its own sleight of hand

Where she goes we go
What we do is made manifest
If the hostess is killed
there is simply nowhere to live

If home is harmed
so are humans
If resources devoured
supply emptied
The earth
she will continue

A rock hurtling through space
Yet what of the miracle
of an ozone layer trapping oxygen
The moon held in earth's gravity
Water sustaining the liquid self
Sunlight giving growth

All treasures of nurturing
All vital for life

The lunacy
destroy what is essential

These gifts freely given
A miraculous convergence of elements
This earth
she does not need us to survive
Yet we need her
Future generations do
Our grandchildren do

I call on you all
Shamans
Earth keepers
Wisdom keepers
Medicine women
Medicine men
Sages
Yogis
Alchemists
Activists
Miracle workers
Healers
All of the light

I call on you, whoever you are
I call on you to raise your hand
I call on you to take action
I call on you to save what is the womb of our mother

Know who you truly are
You are of this earth
You are intrinsically woven
into the tapestry of nature
You are her child
She is your mother

Allow yourself to stumble
Succumb to her affection

Life a sacred encounter as we walk this earth

Become a steward of this earth
A protector of this earth
Become what you were born to be

Be less of a commodity
Take less
Invest more

In dazzling awareness
of what it demands
to sustain the convenience of it all

Unshackle the shame to release right action
Bow to her intimacy with you
until your life with her
becomes a devoted love affair
Sanctified below the current of existence

Remember your birthright
Remember your sovereignty
Remember gratitude
to this place

we all call home

VITA

Miranda

What is my work?
A question still fraught
with the distillation of words
Yet in simple terms, it is my calling
I have been called a guide
I am an author
A poet
A teacher
A mentor
I give counsel
I have been called a mystic
I have been known as a fast track
to distilling of the truth
I listen deeply
I am a lover of truth

Freedom

Respect

I play and dance with energy

I lead people into silence

Into retreats of the energetic realms

My brand is Know Who You Truly Are

Spirit is my boss

I rebel fiercely into acts of service

to weave the sacred into the mundane

www.mirandajbarrett.com

info@mirandajbarrett.com

Ed Bacon

Reverend Ed Bacon is an Episcopal priest and the author of *8 Habits of Love*.

Ed is a vocal advocate for rearticulating a Christianity for the 21st century, which includes the experience of God's divinity in all creation, instead of worshiping the god of fear, separateness, and white male heterosexual Christian supremacy.

He also works to dismantle all forms of systemic bigotry. A leader in interfaith circles and an advocate of science-friendly theology and leadership in anxious times, he teaches contemplative practices, how our oneness in love overcomes our separateness and fear.

He is dedicated to help save the Pando Forest in southern Utah, the largest organism on the planet, which he considers symbolic of the interconnectedness of all creation.

Ed has appeared on a variety of radio and TV shows. Oprah Winfrey recently named him a soul teacher on her SuperSoul 100 list, a collection of 100 awakened leaders who are using their voice to elevate humanity.

www.edbacon.co

Megan Barrett

Megan is a photographer based out of Northern California whose primary focus is to capture the relationship between the ocean and the animals and humans that thrive in it.

Megan has a specific interest in the play of light and water and the texture and colors that come from the intersection of the two. With her background in painting, she tends to rely heavily on this training when composing photos.

In shooting exclusively film, she has learned that intention and consideration are the greatest assets, especially when shooting something as dynamic as the ocean with a camera that takes only thirty-six frames.

To enjoy more photography and order prints go to:

www.meganshootsfilm.com

A FALL INTO GRATITUDE

In the undoing of myself
The offering up of gifts
Giving away the veils of protection
A surrender into vulnerability
Into what makes this life real

As I unharbour the ships of war
Unshackle the armor
To invite the fertile soil of gratitude to set me free

This a return
A pilgrimage home
Back to what belongs
Into all that matters

Within eternal ease
and the nectar of grace
Appreciation effortless in potency

Rejoicing in the glory of recognition
108 poems revealed
A holy number

All I have tried to be
All I have been desperate to become

As the grip is released
The weighted oppression

The tooth's edge
within a shedding of skin
of ever belonging to another

Instead to meet with mercy
Finally at rest the stranger within

This offering of poems scribed into form could not possibly have been birthed without the support, love, and encouragement of some dearly beloved humans in my life.

My deepest gratitude to those precious beings I have sent poems to over the years and who have echoed a heralding that they needed to be shared. Without which I would never have taken this next step.

With a gratitude which makes my heart soar above and beyond words:

My glorious daughter Megan Barrett, whose photos adorn these pages.

And her brilliant and wonderful partner Jack Wolfe Bernstein for keeping it real.

Ed Bacon, a fellow mystic whose foreword roots this book into the hands of God. My heartfelt gratitude.

Birla Angelica, my beloved Scorpio sister whose presence in my life has softened tendrils of my heart-strings by being a living embodiment of fierce kindness always.

Nina Hoffmeirer and Johanna Brandvik. Ancient friendships birthed again in this lifetime.

Lucy Alexander, my oldest dear friend who has witnessed much of this written journey with a love which has endured across time and space and whose editing skills pale my lack of grammar into oblivion.

Miranda Carey, a beloved witness to my life who holds my feet to the fire and encourages authenticity as the flame always worth burning. My love abounds.

Amelia Hoffman, my sister in alms, my sister in blood, my twin orphan of light. My heart implodes with love for you as we bear witness to each other's lives and strike a new chord of our family constellation with fierce devotion.

Rob Floe, who sees beyond the physical and encourages the realms of spirit to unfold. This book being such.

Rod Stryker for his love, dear friendship and whispers of acknowledgment and encouragement in this labor of love.

Marva Brannum, for her love and being a wordsmith of poetic justice in her own right.

Susie Fitch, a passionate crusader for these poems' flight of life.

Bethany Kelly, publisher extraordinaire, for her expertise, patience, and calm loving support.

Adyashanti for affording me the precious gift of silence as a muse for these unfoldings.

David Whyte, a guiding light and inspiration into the piercing realms of poetry.

Alison Armstrong and Jane Goodall, pioneering women whose indomitable spirits and activism inspires hope into action.

Rosalynn Fitz Patrick, a demure sage in therapeutic attire. For teaching me to cradle my shards of pain in a balm of compassion and tenderness I did not even know was possible

James Hood for offering a sanctuary for the witch to live up on the hill in among ancient oak trees as a haven for this creation.

My mother Margaret Crawford, my father Robert Barrett and all my ancestors who gave me the gift of this precious life.

To those of you who have inspired me.

To those of you who love me.

To those of you who tested me.

To those of you who birthed me.

I bow in reverence and gratitude to you.

On bended knee

Allowing this gift of more light to enter.

CHANCE YOUR ARM

A surrender
into the deepening waters of gratitude
A fall back into grace
A collapse of all controlled

A softening of pursed lips
To bestow the gentlest kiss
on the forehead
of all we love

A resonance of gratitude
for this earth we call home

For all the gifts given
utterly undeserved
This miraculous body
The love of another
Solid ground beneath the feet
Air to breathe
Gravity to hold
Offered freely without agenda

While the mind melts into stillness
Thoughts enter
to pause at last in the cave of the heart
Adorned with love
Jeweled with hope

The shadow boxer of fear
The vixen of hate
Laid down to rest
Both a burden too great to bear

The sharp tongue
The insidious beliefs
Dissolved
Absolved
again and again
into a heartfelt
moment upon moment
of thankfulness

for you

OTHER WRITINGS BY MIRANDA

A Woman's Truth
A Life Truly Worth Living

Priceless teachings reveal your transformational journey ahead. Obstacles to self-care are explored as clear and loving intentions are conceived.

The Grandeur of Sleep
Permission to Rest

Miraculous benefits are realized as the worlds of sleep, relaxation, and rejuvenation are explored and deeply honored.

Nourishing Nutrition
Reclaim Your Health and Vitality

Reap the bountiful rewards while eating as nature intended. Claim your health and vitality with these simple, yet powerful tools to nourish and heal your body.

Embodying Movement
Ground Your Whole Being

Discover how to embrace your whole being through the life-enhancing benefits of body movement.

Body Care
Cherish Your Body as a Temple

Learn to honor your extraordinary body as a living temple and listen to the healing messages she whispers.

Feminine Power
Fully Access Your Supreme Birthright

Welcome and reclaim this intrinsic privilege while living in harmonious balance between the masculine and the feminine.

The Abundance of Wealth
Receive the Gifts of Prosperity

Understand the energy flow of prosperity and weave the threads of abundance throughout the tapestry of your life.

Find Your Authentic Voice
The Courage to Express Who You Truly Are

Your greatest ally is born when you courageously speak your truth and claim your unique power.

A Love Affair with the Self
Love Yourself, No Matter What

As you become highly attuned to your own needs, allow love to lead the way. Grant yourself permission to honor and express your heart's truest desires.

Living a Spiritual Life
Ground Your Divinity Here on Earth

Discover what spirituality means to you by consciously living in your Divine essence as you bridge the worlds of the sacred and the mundane.

Service as a Way of Life
Ignite the Fire of Love to Truly Be of Service

By utilizing the gems of exquisite self-care on a daily basis and honoring your truth, your mission of service is born.

The Crowning Glory
Fully Rejoice in Being You

A celebration overflowing with love, blessings, grace, and gratitude. Stand confident within your own truth as your mind becomes of service to your heart.

The Food of Life
The Versatile Vegetable

More than just a cookbook, a comprehensive guide for nourishing your life.

Reiki
The Spirit of Energy

Insightful guidebooks full of wisdom which introduce you to the potent and healing world of Reiki.

Level One Reiki Guidebook

Level Two Reiki Guidebook

Advanced Reiki Guidebook

Master Level Guidebook

The Grandeur of Sleep & Rejuvenating Rest
The ancient healing art of rest and relaxation.

Yoga Nidra, a simple yet profound practice which alleviate stress and tension, allowing your mind, body, and spirit to heal, restore, and replenish.

TO ORDER, PLEASE VISIT:

www.MirandaJBarrett.com
www.Amazon.com

"Howsoever deep your darkness
You are never without me."

CPSIA information can be obtained
at www.ICGtesting.com
Printed in the USA
BVHW012158161221
624260BV00002B/124